First Comes Love,
Then Comes Money

First Comes *Love,* Then Comes MONEY

A Couple's Guide to
Financial Communication

Scott and Bethany Palmer

The Money Couple

HarperOne
An Imprint of HarperCollinsPublishers

HarperOne

This book is written as a source of information only. The information contained in this book should by no means be considered a substitute for the advice, decisions, or judgment of the reader's financial or other professional adviser. All efforts have been made to ensure the accuracy of the information contained in this book as of the date published. The author and the publisher expressly disclaim responsibility for any adverse effects arising from the use or application of the information contained herein.

Names and identifying details of the individuals discussed in this book have been changed to protect their privacy.

Interior Design by Laura Lind Design

FIRST EDITION

Library of Congress Cataloging-in-Publication Data

Palmer, Scott.
First comes love, then comes money : a couple's guide to financial communication / Scott and Bethany Palmer. — 1st ed.
p. cm.
Includes index.
ISBN 978–0–06–164991–2
1. Couples—Finance, Personal. 2. Finance, Personal. 3. Financial security.
I. Palmer, Bethany. II. Title.
HG179.P1888 2009
332.0240086'5—dc22 2009000179

09 10 11 12 13 RRD(H) 10 9 8 7 6 5 4 3 2 1

To every couple that has ever struggled with money, fought over money, worried about money.

May this book help you relieve financial stress and recapture your dreams of the life you want to build together.

Contents

Introduction

*T*he first time I cheated on my wife we ended up without a kitchen. Hi, my name is Scott, and I have committed financial infidelity.

Bethany and I hadn't been married very long when she mentioned that she thought our condo's kitchen needed updating. How I took us from that comment to a completely gutted kitchen in less than four hours is a story we'll tell you a little later. But suffice it to say, it was the first of many moments when we had to decide if we were going to let that costly miscommunication ruin us or help us grow closer. We chose the latter, but just barely.

You've picked up this book either because you're struggling in your financial communication already or you want to prevent financial miscommunication from happening in the first place. OK, maybe you haven't ripped out your kitchen, but perhaps you've hidden your spending from your partner because you'd rather lie than argue about money.

Maybe you've hidden your spending from your partner because you'd rather lie than argue about money.

Or you've decided to maintain separate checking accounts because you don't really trust your partner to keep things balanced. Or you've got a few credit cards your partner doesn't know about because you don't like feeling controlled by someone else. These deceptions, these separations, these secrets are the foundation of financial infidelity.

Financial infidelity is any money decision—a big one, a small one, one you can afford, one you can't—that's made without the knowledge or consent of your partner. That means it doesn't matter if you're sneaking in a double latte every morning even though you and your partner have agreed that your budget only has room for a single, or you're racking up thousands of dollars in debt on a credit card your partner doesn't know you have. Either way, it's financial infidelity.

Conflicts about money are one of the primary reasons relationships end in the United States, and if you've been in a relationship for more than a week, you can probably understand why. Money can tick people off like nothing else. That's because most of us have very strong, deeply ingrained ideas about how and when we use our money—and since money impacts nearly every decision we make in our lives, those ideas come into play several times a day. When those ideas clash, most couples have no idea what to do. And for far too many couples, those collisions lead to financial infidelity.

That's where we come in. As professional financial advisers, we believe that when couples know how to communicate about money, they can prevent those clashing ideas from destroying their relationships. When two people learn how to understand each other, how to talk about money, and how to work together to build a solid financial future, they can put an end to financial infidelity.

We've met with thousands of couples who are in financial trouble. And with very few exceptions, none of them meant for that trouble to start. None of them woke up and said, "Today's the day I'm going to lie to my beloved and destroy our family finances!" Instead, it starts with one half truth, one little betrayal of trust that leads to the next betrayal and the next. The trouble starts with a little miscommunication and ends with two people sitting in our office hardly able to tolerate each other.

Financial infidelity can consume your relationship like a wildfire taking hold in a field of dry grass. You end up spending what seems like every single moment talking about money, fighting about money, crying about money. Or you stop talking about money altogether because it's just too painful. Without solid, healthy financial communication, your relationship is primed for the fire of financial infidelity to take hold.

But it doesn't have to. Consider this book a bucket of water you can use to douse the flames. We're going to show you how to put an end to the financial infidelity in your relationship—whether it's a raging inferno or a tiny ember waiting to ignite. By teaching you some basic—yet essential—financial communication skills, we will help you put out that fire and show you how to let your dreams rise back up from the debris.

This is your chance to join hands, turn around, and march into a new, healthier, stronger life together.

Ready? Let's go.

Getting to Know You All Over *Again*

Chapter One

The Truth About Financial Infidelity

*I*t's the kind of phone call you hope you never get. Shannon,* an acquaintance, called me to ask for help with her finances. "Bethany, I just found out that Michael has gotten us into some serious debt, and I need your help getting out of it."

"What kind of debt are we talking about?" I asked her.

"A little over $30,000," Shannon replied.

It was all I could do not to scream into the phone.

I quickly put on my financial adviser hat and asked her to tell me what had happened. What she said next still makes me want to throttle her husband.

"Well, a few weeks ago I got a call from the video store. They told me we still had one of their movies and that we needed to return it and pay the late fees. I asked them what movie it was and they gave me the name of something that was clearly an adult video. I told them we didn't rent movies like that and that they'd made a mistake. They called back a couple of days later, and I told them the same thing. The guy said, 'Well, then someone stole your credit card because this is

---

* Names and identifying details of the individuals discussed in this book have been changed to protect their privacy.

the account we have in our records.' So I went to the video store to straighten them out. I talked to the manager, and he showed me the signature on the rental agreement. It was Michael's."

Shannon went on to tell me that the devastation she felt at the video store was nothing compared to what she felt next. She went home and started looking through their bills. That's when she learned that her husband, who had been in charge of their finances, was behind on car payments and life insurance payments and had a stack of unpaid credit card bills. Then she landed on a bill for a credit card she didn't know he had, a bill that included charges from pornographic Web sites. She had been lied to for years. It turned out that Michael had been using this card to fund his porn

> *It turned out that Michael had been using this card to fund his porn addiction.*

addiction without Shannon suspecting anything. Here was a marriage filled with betrayal, broken trust, and years of deception. And you know what Shannon and I talked about? Her debt.

I helped Shannon work out a long-term plan for paying off what they owed and for getting their finances back on track. It took about three years and a lot of hard work and sacrifice, but she did it. She got her family out of a financial crisis.

Most financial advisers would say this is a success story. Here was a couple with deep debt, but with hard work and a commitment to live within their budget, they recovered. I was proud of Shannon, and she was proud of herself. "Finally," she told me, "that nightmare is over and we can start fresh."

And guess what? Two years later, Michael has again run up more than $30,000 in credit card debt, back taxes, and loans taken against their retirement fund. Shannon could end up in deep legal trouble because of their tax situation. Her car has been repossessed. They barely speak to each other. Michael sleeps on the couch. Their marriage is a disaster.

Five years ago, Shannon and I both treated this as a purely financial problem. Wrong. The money mess was a symptom of something else. It was a symptom of financial infidelity.

Financial infidelity is what happens when a person drives her family into debt with her overspending. It is the lack of financial planning that leaves couples desperate. It is two people maintaining separate accounts because they don't trust each other enough to pool their resources. It is the desire to control another person's life by limiting his access to money. It is what happens any time a person lies, cheats, or deceives his partner about money. It is a betrayal of the trust that two people put in each other when they commit to a relationship. Overspending, separation, lack of planning, control, and secrets—these forms of financial betrayal can be just as damaging to that trust as sexual betrayal.

We own a financial planning company with tens of thousands of clients all over the world. We work with incredibly wealthy people and people who have almost nothing. And we can tell you that financial infidelity is everywhere. Take a look at these numbers: 51 percent of all marriages in the United States end in divorce. The top cause of divorce? Money.[1] Nearly 75 percent of couples in the United States cite money as the primary cause of their marital fighting.[2] And among financial planners like us, more than 40 percent say money is the primary reason their clients seek divorce. It's the rare couple that doesn't deal with some kind of financial infidelity.

Financial infidelity seldom happens abruptly. It sneaks into a relationship without warning. It creeps in through those little lies, those seemingly harmless secrets that couples have about money. It starts when a guy gets a private credit card. He convinces himself he'll only charge $100 a month. But then the $100 turns into $500 and the $500 into $5,000, and the spiral just keeps swirling down. It starts when a woman tells her partner she spent $50 at the mall instead of the $175 she really dropped because she doesn't want him to get mad at her. It starts when he hides the real depth of the debt he's bringing into the relationship or when she refuses to participate in managing their family finances. Just like sexual infidelity starts with an innocent business lunch or a little flirtation over coffee, financial infidelity begins with that first secret, that first half truth, that first hidden purchase.

> *Financial infidelity begins with that first secret, that first half truth, that first hidden purchase.*

The first betrayal leads to the next and to the next, and before long, the relationship is dying.

Forget the Budget, Save the Relationship

This book isn't going to tell you how to create a balanced budget. It's not going to tell you how to pay off your mortgage in ten years. It's not going to tell you how to live debt free for the rest of your life. Why? Because without healthy financial communication, without a commitment to putting an end to financial infidelity, none of that stuff works. After more than thirty-five years of combined experience as financial advisers, we've learned that if you don't know how to talk about money with your partner, if you don't know how to keep financial infidelity from destroying your relationship, budgets and plans and payments won't mean squat.

The conventional wisdom out there is that financial health comes from a clear budget, minimal debt, and controlled spending. So when couples hit a financial bump, they head to the bookstore to find a resource that will give them the perfect road map to financial freedom. They create tidy budgets. They pay off their debt. They control their spending.

Those road maps are fine and they often get people where they want to be—at least on paper. But like any road map, they don't take into account the fact that there are people driving the car, people with their own personalities and habits. Maps can show you the route to your destination, but they can't help you get there without yelling at the person riding shotgun.

That's why even couples with perfect budgets and paid-off houses and zero debt still end up arguing about money, angry about money, resentful about money. Even couples with spotless credit reports can be mired in the kind of financial infidelity that sullies relationships. Because the budget isn't the problem; the lack of financial communication is the problem.

We didn't get that for a long time. Bethany and I used to talk with couples having serious financial problems. We'd put together the cash flow worksheet, help them develop a budget, create a plan for paying off their debt, and send them on their way. We'd feel like we'd done our job and helped these nice people. They'd feel good because they'd taken this important step toward getting their finances on track. And then we'd get the phone calls: "He blew our budget!" "She's not following the rules!" "This isn't working!"

Those same couples we'd tried to help would show up six months later to discuss their assets in preparation for their divorce. We'd ask them what happened, and one of them would say, "She's just not committed to this budget." But what these men and women were really saying was, "My partner is just not committed to this relationship."

We began to realize that our question shouldn't have been, why isn't the budget working? It should have been, why isn't this financial relationship working? Because in nearly every financial crisis we see, the credit cards aren't the problem and the mortgage isn't the problem. They are symptoms of the financial communication that isn't happening. And when that communication isn't there, financial infidelity almost certainly is.

If you're not convinced that financial communication is the key to preventing and recovering from financial infidelity, consider this glimpse into life with the Palmers. The house we live in was pre-wired for a home theater. We agreed that we ought to get a new TV and sound system so we could have some serious family movie nights (OK, I did think a little bit about how great *Gladiator* and *Monday Night Football* would be in surround sound).

As we talked about how much we'd spend, my mind spun through all the cool things we could do with this great system. So when Bethany said, "OK, we're agreed on the budget, right?" I *heard* the number, but it didn't really register. I just nodded as I grabbed my keys and headed for the car.

When I got to the store, I met a helpful fellow named Danny. I told him what I was looking for. Danny's eyes lit up as he said, "I've got just the thing."

Danny and I spent two hours strolling the aisles. During our tour he was patient enough to explain to me why the entry-level cheap stuff would break down and need lots of repair. He pointed out that those systems didn't have enough wattage to produce the effect I was looking for. He then ushered me into a dark room where the movie *Top Gun* was playing. "Listen to this," he said, grabbing a remote and punching a few buttons.

The next two minutes were magical. Tom Cruise flew his F-14 right beside me. I swear the hair on my arms moved in the wind he created. "Yes," I shouted to Danny over the flybys. "This is the one I want. My wife will love it!"

We grabbed two flatbed carts and stacked them with all the equipment I'd need. We had speakers, woofers, subwoofers, tweeters, receivers, remotes, tuners, and about sixteen miles of speaker wire. Danny told me what a great deal I was getting. He even gave me a discount and threw in the protection plan. I was all smiles as the perky checkout girl scanned my loot. She finished and said, "Mr. Palmer, that'll be $5,027.78. Would you like to put that on your Visa?"

Yeah. This wasn't going to go over too well.

When I got home, I had Bethany close her eyes while I lugged in every box. Five trips to the car later, I told her to open her eyes. Before she could speak, I rambled off all the reasons why this tower of boxes was necessary. I told her about the discount, the quality of the system, Danny the salesman, and even the perky checkout girl. But instead of getting excited about my triumphant purchase, she looked at me and said as calmly as she could, "Exactly how much did you spend?"

The next couple of hours were some of the ugliest I've ever experienced. I had violated a money rule, to be sure. But I had also violated our financial relationship. We'd made a decision together, and I went off on my own and acted like our marriage didn't matter as much as a subwoofer.

But as awful as I felt when I confessed I'd spent five times the amount we'd agreed to, and as angry as Bethany was, we faced my mistake together. I admitted I was stupid, knowing that even though she agreed, Bethany wasn't going to stab me in the eye with a fork at dinner. Instead, we worked together to figure out what happened and what we could do about it. The next day I returned more than half the stuff I'd bought. I didn't feel cheated out of my cool system by my nag of a wife. I felt loved and forgiven and understood by my partner. There was a big problem, but we have learned how to communicate about our finances in a way that allows us to solve the problem and move on. My act of financial infidelity didn't destroy us. We recovered from it and learned from it.

We surveyed hundreds of couples about their financial communication, and they told us their stories—you'll hear from a number of these couples as we work through the book. Some stories are incredibly inspiring. Others make you wonder how the couple has managed to stay together. Some couples told us about big, blatant betrayals like the one Shannon experienced. Others offered examples of more subtle forms of financial infidelity. In some ways, those subtle problems can be even more damaging to a relationship than the big blowups. Take this story for example:

> *Some couples told us about big, blatant betrayals.*

One woman, Holly, wrote, "Early in our marriage, my husband bought a travel mug. A friend of his had one that he liked, so he went out and bought the same kind. When I found out he paid $35 for it, I was furious! He didn't even bother to find out if it was a good buy—which it was not—or even to talk to me about it! As a result, we began to give each other a monthly allowance to be spent any way we want without input from the other person. This has eliminated bickering, and we are both more conservative knowing that once the monthly allowance is gone, that's it."

On the surface, this sounds like a great solution. But look at the exclamation points Holly uses. You can feel her lingering irritation over a mug her husband bought *years* ago. It wasn't a good buy, and he didn't clear it with her. Seriously, it was $35, and if she still needs exclamation points to tell us about it, you can bet she still uses them when she reminds her husband about it—something we're pretty certain she does. He spent $35 on something that made him happy, and she's never let him forget it. This couple solved their money problem.

But the relationship? Probably not so great. Her husband may have committed financial infidelity long ago, but this couple's—particularly Holly's—inability to participate in healthy financial communication and move on has most likely caused lasting damage to their marriage.

It's certainly true that it feels good to pay off your mortgage. And it's great to create a budget and live within your means. But if living by that budget causes you to berate or resent your partner, what's the point? You might not have any debt, but if you've avoided debt by never taking a family vacation or creating any family memories, who cares? You can pay cash for all your cars, but if you haven't made love in two years, so what? We'd rather see couples with $15,000 in credit card debt who love each other and are working together to get to a better place than a husband and wife who have no credit card debt but a treasure trove of resentment and bitterness.

We're not therapists, but our work still gives us the opportunity to see couples at their best and at their worst. Over and over, we talk with couples for whom money issues are signs of much deeper struggles. These couples have lost crucial pieces of their relationship. They've lost the ability to compromise, and they've lost the ability to offer grace. And compromise and grace are the keystones of healthy financial communication.

We meet a lot of couples who think they're compromising. They tell us about their separate checking accounts and their allowances. One person gives up control of the finances in the name of compromise. But none of this is compromise. More often than not, separate checking accounts and allowances and singular control are a sure sign that two people are leading separate lives. They suggest a relationship where no one is willing to give up control, where financial communication has broken down so completely that it's just easier to stop talking about money altogether.

There's also a terrible loss of grace in these types of marriages. Couples get to the point where their financial resentments and mistrust run so deep that there is no forgiveness. These are the relationships in which $35 coffee mugs still create intense irritation. One woman we know, Susan, spent twenty minutes sitting in our offices scolding her husband for spending their retirement money on a land deal that ended up falling apart. We asked when that happened and she told us it was twenty-five years prior. Susan went on to rail about how they never recovered from his ridiculous mistake. And we wanted to say, "No, *you* never recovered. Get over it!"

Successful financial relationships include room for failure and mistakes. So when we hear spouses beat each other up with shame and guilt and flat-out ridicule, we know their marriage is likely heading for financial infidelity and—sadly—a terrible divorce.

It's a whole lot easier to make money the problem; when you focus on the money, you don't have to get into the tough stuff, the relational issues, that can be incredibly painful to deal with. But we believe that when couples are willing to dig into these issues, when they hold hands and face these battles together, they come out so much stronger. And not just financially.

Your money problems aren't about money; they are about financial miscommunication.

If you learn nothing else from this book, we want you to learn this: Your money problems aren't about money; they are about financial miscommunication.

The amount of debt you have or don't have, the amount of savings you have or don't have, are beside the point. And these struggles aren't limited to people with a lot of money. They aren't limited to people with very little money. Problems communicating about money have nothing to do with economics, gender, race, or age. If you and your partner don't know how to have constructive, respectful conversations about money, you are in danger of falling deeper and deeper into financial infidelity.

Here's what we mean. Our first home as a couple was a rundown condo in a good neighborhood. We knew we wouldn't live in it forever, but we still wanted it to be a nice home. We'd talked in a general way about fixing it up. The kitchen in particular needed some serious help, so we'd hired a painter to paint the cabinets, thinking it might do the job. It didn't.

One afternoon Bethany and her grandmother were getting ready to go shopping. As the three of us stood in the kitchen, Bethany said, "We really have to do something about this kitchen." And off they went.

Within half an hour, I had the cabinets pulled off the walls. By the time Bethany and her grandmother came home three hours later, all that was left were a few pipes coming up through the subfloor. I had gutted the whole thing—the counters gone, the floor ripped up, the appliances out. I was very proud of myself.

Bethany, on the other hand, was . . . well, let's just say she didn't react with the level of enthusiasm I'd hoped for. I had committed financial infidelity because I made a financial decision without her input. (Well, I kind of thought I had her input, but as she silently surveyed my work in the kitchen, it was pretty clear that I had really misread her comment.)

My afternoon of manliness forced us to make a series of financial decisions we weren't prepared to make. We remodeled the kitchen, and it looked great. But the shiny new kitchen made the carpet in the living room look pretty dingy. So out it went! Once the new carpet was in, the walls seemed dull. You can probably predict the ending here. Within six months, we had a gorgeous condo. And a Dumpster load of debt—$35,000 in debt, to be exact.

But what we did next is what makes our story of financial infidelity very different from Shannon and Michael's story. The numbers are the same, but one is about a devastating pattern of financial infidelity. The other is about what can happen when a couple knows how to communicate about money.

Our kitchen story could have ended very badly. Bethany could have ripped into me about how my impulsive teardown had pushed us into this huge debt. I could have thrown the blame right back by reminding her that her suggestion that we do something was what got me going in the first place. We could have treated the debt as the problem. But instead, we saw our miscommunication for what it was, looked at our credit card bills, looked at each other, and said, "What are we going to do about this?"

We're not perfect by any means. We can—and do—flub this up. But we believe that good financial communication can mean the difference between a marriage in which we have a great story to tell about how I tore out the kitchen, and a marriage in which we're sitting in some lawyer's office divvying up our assets.

Not Your Financial Planner's Advice

Here's the good news: We believe that no matter how bad things are in your relationship, no matter how deep the financial infidelity has run, you can recapture the life you want to have together. But we also believe it will take some serious work to do that. And that's what this book is for.

We're going to ask you to make some hard decisions and have some hard conversations. We're going to ask you to let go of hurt and anger that you might have been holding on to for decades. And we're going to ask you to reframe your ideas about what it means to be in a partnership.

Marriage experts often encourage couples to think of themselves as a team. But we don't think that's the best approach. I'm a big football fan—Bethany might say I border on obsessive—and I love a great game. But there's one guy I always feel sorry for: the guy who loses the game for the team.

He might be the kicker who misses the field goal in the clutch. He might be the quarterback who fumbles on the one with five seconds on the clock. He might be the tackle who lets the guy through for the make-or-break first down. Whoever it is, this is for sure: Every fan knows his name, and every fan hates him until he redeems himself. He's remembered for his one failure. He's "that guy." It's not the team that takes the hit, it's that guy.

But partnerships work differently. Partners have to communicate. They have to make decisions together. If they don't, they both fail. One person doesn't take the hit, the partnership does. Partnerships depend on connection, openness, and respect. If one partner decides not to play by those rules, the partnership simply can't survive.

It's when that sense of partnership disintegrates that couples end up in financial—and relational—tailspins. Once trust, respect, and communication have given way to deceit, indifference, and secrets, that partnership has become little more than two people who happen to live in the same house. And nothing seems to engender deceit, indifference, and secrecy quite as quickly as money.

That's because money touches every single part of life—where we live, what we do, what we wear, where we eat, what we eat, what we drive, who our friends are, and on and on. Our attitudes about money impact every decision we make—what kind of shampoo we use, how long our showers are, what we have for breakfast. And that's before we even get out the door. So when couples talk about money issues, they are really talking about life, period. Which is why people get defensive about their spending, why they don't want anyone else to tell them how and what they can do with their money, why they resist being completely honest about their financial lives. But if you want your financial relationship to work, if you want money to become something that helps you live the life you want rather than the source of endless tension, then it's time to grab your partner by the hand and step into the future, together.

> *Our attitudes about money impact every decision we make.*

The tools in this book will only work if you and your partner agree, right now, that you are ready to change your lives. You will both need to read the book—it won't work if one person just tells the other one what to do and why he needs to change. True partnership involves both partners sharing the responsibility and moving toward change. So make a decision right now to work through the advice in this book together.

The book is divided into three sections. The first section will help you and your partner discover and understand your money personalities. You'll find out how you think about and treat money. Then you will look at the ways these money personalities can conflict. So often, this is where financial infidelity begins—two people think about money in completely different ways and simply can't figure out how to communicate. We'll show you how to use your money personalities to build a true partnership that brings out the best in each of you.

Understanding and appreciating your money personalities is the first step in recovering from and preventing financial infidelity. The next step is to get serious about uncovering that infidelity. We'll guide you through that process with a profile called the Financial Relationship Index. This profile will help you figure out exactly where financial infidelity is showing up in your relationship. We know this sounds like a frightening prospect—and it kind of is. But figuring this out, making a commitment to being honest, and stepping into your future with a clean slate is the only way to make a fresh start with your financial relationship.

Finally, the third section of this book will give you three basic financial communication tools you will use to guard yourselves against future financial infidelity. You'll find out how to fight fair, make a plan for prioritizing your financial issues, and start working together during a monthly Money Huddle. These tools will get you moving forward, but they'll also give you a solid framework for building financial communication that truly works.

There's not a relationship that can't be saved, and there's not a budget that can't be reworked if you arm yourself with the right tools. We know couples who fell apart financially—couples who could hardly look at each other—who have found the strength and commitment to rethink their financial communication in order to repair their relationship. We know couples who feel like failures because they can't make that best-selling budgeting plan work, only to realize that the budget isn't really the problem.

We believe you can change your financial picture. More importantly, we believe you can have the relationship you always wanted, one filled with a shared vision for the future. But you have to decide right now that you believe it too. You have to decide you are ready to start thinking differently about finances and take back your relationship. You have to look your partner in the eye and decide that you are ready to let go of old hurts and to grab on to hope.

SOMETHING TO TALK ABOUT

At the end of each chapter, you'll find a question to spark conver-
sation between you and your partner. You might find that some of
them make you laugh and some of them make you argue, but all
of them will help you start talking about money in ways that feel
like a natural extension of your relationship.

What's the craziest story you've ever heard about another
couple's financial infidelity?

Chapter Two

Discovering Your Money Personality

*W*e've met with thousands of couples who are caught in the grip of financial infidelity. One woman told us, "My husband had an ex-wife who, after many years, came back to him demanding more money. He spoke with our attorney regarding this and came to an arrangement for full, complete, and final payment. However, I found out about this only when she called the house with a question about their 'deal.' I confronted him, and he said he didn't want to worry me and that he handled it on his own. I asked him how he would have felt if I'd used our money to pay off someone else. It made me feel unimportant and incompetent, like he didn't think my input on a financial issue was relevant." The secrecy, the sneakiness, the lack of communication in this situation are all hallmarks of financial infidelity.

Here's what another woman had to say about her husband's financial infidelity: "Several times I encouraged my husband to take over the finances of the family. However, it soon came to light that he was unable to handle it. One time he neglected to pay the mortgage because he had overspent and then secretly made arrangements with the mortgage company to cover his mistake. We had so many fights because he feels like he needs to hide the truth from me. He finally came to me and asked me to take back the financial management. I have, but I get weary from carrying this load. But it's much better, I guess."

Or how about this comment from one of our surveys: "We are currently separated due to miscommunication about money."

We'd guess that when you read those stories you recognize a little of yourselves—you wouldn't be reading this book if you had this all figured out. Still, we believe you can find your way back to a relationship where money isn't a cause for hiding and cheating and arguing. We believe it because we've seen couples like these recover. But only when they are willing to stop the lying, the hiding, the controlling, the secrecy, and all the other big and little acts of financial infidelity and replace them with the compromise, grace, respect, and understanding that make for healthy financial communication.

You wouldn't be reading this book if you had this all figured out.

We all want strong, healthy, loving relationships. And when it comes to your financial relationship, the only way to get there is to understand that you and your partner aren't just having random disagreements about money, but rather disagreements rooted in the essence of who each of you are. We call this part of you your money personality. Everybody has one.

In our work with couples struggling with financial infidelity, we often find that at the core of their problems is a fundamental lack of understanding regarding their ideas about money. All they know is that money creates problems for them. What they don't know is why. And as we've tried to figure out how to help these couples learn to communicate about their finances, we've come to see that everyone has a particular money personality that shapes how they think about, feel about, and talk about money. When those thoughts and feelings and conversations clash with the thoughts and feelings and conversations of another person, it can feel like the whole relationship is falling apart.

But understanding and respecting your partner's money personality can help you get to the heart of your money conflicts—and therefore to the heart of financial infidelity. Consider this man who wrote, "I came from a wealthy family; my wife didn't. Early in our marriage, there was a lot of tension between us, and we didn't know why. We thought there was something wrong with our marriage, that we were no longer enjoying or appreciating each other. We didn't realize that tension was coming from our different attitudes about money. We finally decided we had to talk about whatever it was that was going on between us. We discovered that the real problem was our different experiences and attitudes about money. We had to learn to understand each other's position and respect it. We found common ground. It was a great start to forty-eight years of marriage."

When we meet with couples, both partners think their financial problems would go away if the other person would just shape up and start being reasonable. If that other person would just *change*, everything would be fine. But your money personality is as much a part of you as your hair color or your love of pizza. You can cover it up, you can even learn to curb it a bit, but your money personality just doesn't change.

When couples take the time to identify, talk about, and understand their money personalities, it blows the doors off of all kinds of financial relationship problems. It's like earning a Ph.D. in your partner. No relationship can grow or deepen without both partners studying each other and continually rediscovering each other. Understanding your partner's money personality is a crucial part of that process, so when you figure out why your partner thinks about money the way he does, when you realize that your partner's perspective has as much value as yours, you are on your way to a truly satisfying financial future. You *get* each other in a whole new way.

At the end of the day, understanding your partner's money personality helps you develop a sense of empathy for this person you love and share your life with. That empathy is the key to dealing with the financial conflicts that happen in all relationships. Later in the book, we'll talk about those conflicts and how to work through them in a way that doesn't damage your relationship. But doing that actually starts right here. It starts with seeing your partner with new eyes, a new sense of why she thinks about money the way she does. It involves a willingness to step into your partner's shoes—even in the midst of an argument—to see things from his perspective for a moment. When you have that kind of empathy for and understanding of your partner's money personality, you are well on your way to putting an end to financial infidelity.

The Money Personalities

In this chapter, we'll focus on the five money personalities and the parts they play in financial infidelity.[1] Your goal for the chapter is to identify your money personality and have your partner do the same. We'll use this information throughout the book as we talk about developing better financial communication. In Chapter 3, we'll cover the ways these money personalities interact—the points of conflict and the points of connection.

After working with thousands of couples over the years, we've determined that people have the following money personalities:

The Saver: These are the penny-pinchers of the world. They hate parting with their money and believe just about everything is overpriced. If a Saver finds a buck in her coat pocket, she leaves it there.

The Spender: Spenders love to buy, buy, buy. Some like to buy for themselves; some like to buy for others. But money never sticks around too long for a Spender. If a Spender finds a buck in his coat pocket, he runs to Starbucks to see what he can buy.

The Risk Taker: The entrepreneurs, the inventors, the people on the cover of *Fortune* magazine? All Risk Takers. They aren't afraid of losing everything if it gets them closer to having everything.

The Security Seeker: If you know a planner, you know a Security Seeker. They like knowing their financial future is locked in. They can tell you how much is in their retirement account, how much life insurance they have, and all the reasons why both of those are very good ideas.

The Flyer: If you're a Flyer, you're probably being forced to read this book by your partner. That's because Flyers just don't think about money. We call them Flyers because they fly by the seat of their pants when it comes to financial planning. In other words, there is no plan.

We'll go into more detail about these money personalities in a moment. But before we do, we want you to think about some aspects of this section:

1) You and your partner should both read this chapter. If you have a reasonably good relationship, you might have fun going over the money personalities together and talking about which ones fit each of you. If things are a little rocky for you right now, you might want to read them on your own, have your partner do the same, then talk about what you've discovered over dinner some night when the time feels right.

   Here's why: The descriptions that follow include some of the challenges of each money personality. And these challenges can be hard to read about, much less own up to. It's a lot easier to accept those parts of yourself when you feel like they are acceptable to someone else, so it's important to approach this section carefully. But if you and your partner read through these descriptions and use them to blame each other for past financial problems, this whole process will get derailed. We also want to make sure that each of you determines your money personalities for yourselves. These aren't meant to be labels you slap on your partner. They are descriptions of a part of the personality that is real and meaningful to each person. The last thing we want is for couples to start stereotyping each other.

2) You'll likely find that you resonate with more than one of the money personalities. Everyone has a primary money personality, but everyone also has a secondary money personality. The primary money personality is the one that has the most influence on your thoughts and feelings about financial issues. But we've been surprised at how often a couple's conflicts can arise from their secondary money personalities. We are a perfect example of that kind of conflict. Bethany and I share the same primary money personality: the Spender. So when we found ourselves arguing about money, we couldn't figure out why we were having a problem. We were the same! Then we went back to these descriptions and realized that we weren't just Spenders. We each zoomed in on one of the other personalities as well. It turns out Bethany is a Risk Taker, and I'm a Security Seeker. Bam! That's why Bethany gets all excited about wild investment deals and I get nervous. And when two people have such strong—and competing—emotional responses to the same issue, financial communication can break down. Fast.

3) As with any personality inventory, there will be shades of gray here. Very few people live out their money personality in every situation. So when you look at the money personalities, focus on your normal impulses—if spending money gives you a rush, you're probably a Spender, even if your financial situation means you hardly ever buy anything. If buying something at 75 percent off retail makes you giddy, you're probably a Saver, even if what you're buying is a pair of $600 Prada calfskin loafers.

4) Money personalities have nothing to do with economic status, race, gender, or age. They are who you are, regardless of how much money you have, how old you are, or how you grew up. The goal for now is to find yourself on this list and start thinking about how your money personality impacts your attitudes and assumptions about financial issues.

We love helping people discover their money personalities. It's like showing them a part of themselves that they knew was there but had never named before. Once people find their money personalities, all of their spending habits (or lack-of-spending habits), their fears about money, and their fights about money start to make sense. And when two partners figure this out together, they begin to see arguments about money in a different light. Instead of thinking that the other person is just an idiot, they recognize that their partner has a different money personality, one that is just as valid as their own.

The money personalities play a major role in putting an end to financial infidelity. We find that money personalities are often at the

root of behaviors such as secret spending, lack of planning, controlling, overspending, and living separate financial lives. Sometimes
it's a person's own money personality that leads to these patterns.

> *The money person-
> alities play a major
> role in putting an
> end to financial
> infidelity.*

Other times, they show up in response
to the partner's money personality.
Either way, these are the behaviors that
make up financial infidelity. Once you
understand your money personalities,
you and your partner can start changing those behaviors and repairing your
financial relationship.

The Saver

Jim is a major Saver. He'd rather wear his winter coat while he watches
TV in the basement than turn up the heat. He'd rather drive twenty
minutes to shop at the big membership store where he can save a buck
on a gallon of milk than pick it up at the grocery store two blocks from
his house. His wife told us she hesitates to buy him gifts for his birthday
or Christmas. She said, "I know the first thing he thinks about is how
much I paid for that sweater or those tickets or that book. It doesn't
even matter if I get something on sale or if he really loves it. He can't
stop thinking about the money I spent. I like giving him gifts, but he
rarely enjoys them. It's gotten to the point where my 'gift' to him is not
buying anything. It kind of takes the fun out of holidays."

It's easy to recognize a Saver. He's the lawyer who drives a fifteen-
year-old car. She's the coworker who always packs a lunch and brings
day-old doughnuts to the coffee break. But when you are a Saver, you
don't necessarily know it. That's because for a Saver, saving money is
the most reasonable, rational way to live. It doesn't seem like a personality trait; it seems like common sense.

All Savers have their thing, the little ways they like to save money. For some it's clipping coupons—we know a woman who spends two hours every Sunday poring through the paper to get a $1.50 off this and $0.20 off that. Other Savers refuse to shop anywhere but thrift stores. Still others spend a lot of money on clothes or cars or vacations, but only when they know they're getting a really great deal.

While Savers don't always save in the same ways, some traits are common to most Savers. You're a Saver if you:

- **Get a genuine rush from saving money.** It's a source of pride to get something you wanted for less. A Saver will vacation in Hawaii, but only when she has the frequent flier miles to make the trip. She'll eat every meal in her hotel room so she doesn't have to waste money on restaurants. The vacation part is nice, but it's the doing-it-on-the-cheap part that gets her really excited.

- **Are organized, responsible, and trustworthy when it comes to finances.** Savers know how much money is coming in and how much is going out—in great detail. Savers won't tap out the kids' college fund to pay for a new boat. Savers won't toss a twenty into the office basketball pool.

- **Rarely spend impulsively.** Savers are great at researching a purchase—especially big-ticket items like cars and vacations. They will scour the Internet for deals, plan every detail of a vacation, and make sure they have the money in hand before making a purchase.

- **Avoid credit card debt like head lice.** Savers hate paying interest. They have a visceral reaction to the idea of debt. They want to pay off every bill, in full, right away.

- **Are patient about purchases.** Savers are willing to wait—sometimes for years—to get a good deal. They will even go without basic necessities if they know they can get them for less in a week or two.

- **Know how to prioritize your spending.** If there's something a Saver wants—a trip to Italy, a motorcycle, a paid-off mortgage—he'll scrimp and save on other parts of his budget to make it happen. If she wants to pay off a student loan or eliminate her debt, she will eat nothing but Ramen noodles for a year to make it happen.

Of course, each money personality also has its challenges. If there is stress in your financial relationship, it is most likely the result of these challenges. Knowing what these challenges are—and doing your best to work on them—can go a long way toward strengthening your money communication and nipping financial infidelity in the bud.

If you're a Saver, you need to be aware that you can be:

- **A joy stealer.** A Saver might get all excited about getting in and out of Disneyland without spending any money on food or souvenirs, but unless everyone else in the family is a Saver too, there's going to be some resentment back at the campground (What, you thought this guy was going to spring for a hotel?). If you're a Saver and your partner isn't, your resistance to spending money can create a relationship in which your partner feels like she needs to spend in secret in order to do or have the things that give her joy without upsetting you.

- **Overly focused on financial goals.** Often, the reason Savers are joy stealers is that they tend to only think about the money. So while the rest of the family is making memories on the Matterhorn, Saver Dad is tallying up the day's expenses and hoping they have enough bread left in the tent to make sandwiches again that night. It's great to have firm financial goals and to work hard to meet them, but sometimes Savers need to swallow their anxiety and let themselves—and others—just enjoy life. If they don't, they can easily become controlling, allowing their fears about not having enough money push aside the feelings and needs of the people they love. The Saver might start giving her partner an allowance so she can control how much he spends. Or he might set up his own bank account to make sure his partner can't access all their money.

- **Obsessive about money.** Savers love to talk about money, think about money, and worry about money. They check the stock market every morning. They tell people how much they paid for their clothes. They want to know how much other people paid for their stuff—and can get pretty judgmental when they think it's too much. That judgment can make it hard for the Saver's partner to be honest about his spending. The money obsession can also get so annoying to the Saver's partner that she no longer wants to be part of financial conversations. And that leads to financial separation and secrets.

- **Cheap.** Most Savers have a hard time parting with their money, so much so that they come across as cheap and even selfish to other people. They rarely offer to pay for someone's meal, cringe at pitching in on a group gift, and would rather eat stale sandwiches alone at their desks than join friends for lunch at a restaurant. If the rest of the Saver's family gets just as excited about living on the

cheap, great. But when the Saver insists that others live
her way—even when they have other ideas—she becomes
the kind of control freak no one wants to deal with.

The Spender

Shelley is a typical Spender. She lives in a modest house with her
husband and three children, but she works at a bookstore in a very
trendy, upscale neighborhood. Every day she sees women in beautiful
clothes, toting their equally well-dressed children, buying books and
stationery and little gifties with abandon. Shelley sees all of this as the
norm, so she shops at the same boutiques these women shop at, buys
her children darling outfits from exclusive children's stores, and loves
to shower her friends with trinkets she picks up at the classy gift store
down the street. She loves how she looks, she loves the compliments
her children receive, and she loves how great her friends feel when she
surprises them with beaded purses and handmade silver earrings.

The problem is that none of this fits in the family budget. Every
month, she and her husband look at their bills and wonder how on
earth they managed to spend so much. And Shelley honestly doesn't
know. In true Spender fashion, she doesn't add up the total in her
head while she's shopping; she just shops. She's not thinking about
the budget when she picks out the perfect scarf for her mother-in-
law; she's thinking about how beautiful it will look. Her husband has
tried giving her an allowance, putting her in charge of the books, and
hiding her credit cards, but nothing seems to work. Shelley continues
to ignore the budget she's agreed to and to spend what she wants,
when she wants.

In the interest of full disclosure, you need to know that Scott
and I are both Spenders. And we *love* being Spenders. Even if we
weren't Spenders ourselves, we've met enough of them to know that

Spenders are the life of the party, the ones you love to go out with. They look good. They are great gift-givers. They are spontaneous and generous and a blast to be around.

That's not to say Spenders are necessarily rich. We know plenty of Spenders who have very little money, so instead of heading to Nordstrom, they head to the dollar store and stock up on funny gifts for their buddies. Or they hit the garage-sale circuit every Saturday in search of little treasures. Spenders don't care how *much* they spend or who they spend on. They just like spending. You're a Spender if you:

- **Live in the moment.** Spenders are focused on what's happening right now. Her girlfriends invite her to Vegas for the weekend? She's in. His kids want to head to a water park for the afternoon? Done. So they might have less down the road—for the Spender, that's a small price to pay for making great memories today.

- **Love to buy things for other people.** Spenders get a lot of joy out of giving gifts, helping out, and treating other people. We know a couple—both Spenders—who heard about a family in their community that needed a washer and dryer. They didn't think twice about heading to the home improvement store to get a set for this other family. Could they afford it? Not necessarily. But they love buying and giving and knew they could figure out the money part later.

- **Get a thrill from the purchase.** It doesn't matter if you're shopping at Saks or at the Salvation Army Thrift Store. You just love to spend. A Saver and a Spender can both head to the secondhand store and both get really excited about being there. But the Saver is juiced about the deal, while the Spender loves making the purchase. The price doesn't matter. It's the fun of buying that counts.

It's hard for us to admit this, but we must acknowledge that the Spender money personality does have its challenges. Financial infidelity can easily sneak into the Spender's relationship when he hides or lies about purchases. If you are a Spender, you need to be aware that you can be:

- **Impractical.** Spenders are often impulse buyers. A Spender walks into a store without lists, without limits. Everything at SuperTarget is on his radar. And that means he might come home with groceries, but also a new set of mixing bowls, a throw pillow, and gifts for three babies who haven't even been conceived yet. Spenders rarely calculate how much they can spend on something. They don't do research to find a good deal, and they don't wait for a sale. If they want something, they get it. And *want* is a pretty loose word. Spenders don't differentiate between wants and needs. Because Spenders get such a rush from spending, they can quickly talk themselves into needing just about anything. Like Shelley in the story above, Spenders will sometimes ignore the budget agreements they've made with their partners just because they want something. Not only does that violate the trust in the relationship, it can lead the Spender to become secretive about her purchases or even start lying to her partner about her spending to avoid having to explain her actions.

- **Noncommunicative.** All that impractical impulse buying means Spenders don't think—much less talk—through purchases with their partner. By the time the issue comes up—usually when the credit card bill gets opened—the Spender has moved on to the next thing, so talking about something he bought two weeks ago seems like a waste of time. This lack of communication can come across as secretive and sneaky to the Spender's partner. And sometimes, the Spender *is* being intentionally secretive. Here again, because Spenders would prefer not to talk about what they spend, they might lie about purchases, hide their spending, even get secret credit cards so they don't have to answer to their partners. And that's some serious financial infidelity.

- **Filled with regret.** With two Spenders in our relationship, Christmas is a blast. We get great stuff for each other, cool toys for our kids, and have a wonderful holiday. But January 15 is never pretty. The regret we feel is different from the buyer's remorse of a Saver. We don't regret the purchases or the fun we had buying them and giving them, but we regret getting carried away. If there's only one Spender in the relationship, this regret can lead to more secrets as the Spender scrambles to figure out how to deal with the aftermath of a spending spree.

- **A budget breaker.** Spenders can put together a mean budget, and they can have great intentions of sticking to it. But Spenders rarely do. That can lead them—and their unwitting partners—into serious, life-altering debt. They might even feel bad about overspending, but they have a hard time stopping themselves. This can be unbearably frustrating to the Spender's partner. It sends a pretty clear message that whatever agreements have been made, they have no real meaning for the Spender, a message that can shut

down financial communication, drive the Spender's partner
to resort to all kinds of controlling behavior, and make the
relationship a breeding ground for financial infidelity.

The Risk Taker

Todd is a major Risk Taker. He built his own business from the ground
up, and now he's trying to figure out what's next.

Todd ran on the cross-country team in college and worked part
time in a sporting goods store to help pay his way through school. He
knew that with his love and knowledge of the running world and all
he was learning about marketing and sales at his job, he could start a
line of running stores. So once he graduated, he talked to his parents,
found a few other investors among their friends, and opened a small
running store in his hometown. Ten years later, he's got four stores
around the state. He's been so successful that one of the major sporting goods chains is considering buying him out and making his stores
an offshoot of their bigger stores.

But Todd's not so sure. He could make a ton of money off the
buyout, but he doesn't really want to work for a big company. He likes
being his own boss, and even though all the pressure and risk sits on
his shoulders, he would rather not answer to someone else.

Todd's wife wants him to take the deal. He's worked his tail off
for ten years, and she wants him to take a break, see if they can start a
family, and maybe rid themselves of the worry that comes with being
small business owners. But Todd doesn't want a break. He loves what
he's doing and wants to keep doing it—bigger, better, and on his own.
And in a move that's the very definition of financial infidelity, that's
exactly what he plans to do, regardless of what his wife says.

Donald Trump, Bill Gates, Steve Forbes. Name the richest people
in the United States and you've named a batch of Risk Takers. This is

the money personality of the entrepreneurs of the world, the people who know that the fastest way to wealth is to take chances with your money. Every one of the people on that list has suffered financial losses because of those chances. But clearly, some of those risks paid off.

> *Name the richest people in the United States and you've named a batch of Risk Takers.*

Not every Risk Taker is wealthy. And not every Risk Taker ends up with more successes than failures. There are plenty of Risk Takers who end up bankrupt and broke. But like the other money personalities, this one isn't about how much money a person has, it's about how she thinks about her money.

For Risk Takers, the thrill doesn't just come from the results of their risks, it comes from the risks themselves. Even if they never hit it big, Risk Takers will keep doing what they do. It's just how they're wired. If you're a Risk Taker, you:

- **Are a conceptual thinker.** Risk Takers aren't worried about details. They don't get hung up on the how of an idea. Instead, they get a lead on something—a business opportunity, an investment option, a real estate deal—and they move. Fast. So when a couple of college students come up with a way for people to find what they want on the Internet, it's the Risk Taker who helps them get started. A few years and a few shares of Google stock later, the details hardly matter.

- **Get excited by possibility.** Bethany is a Risk Taker, and sometimes she gets more excited about the idea of something than the thing itself. When she told me about a land development opportunity she wanted us to invest in, there was a gleam in her eye and a quiver in her voice. She was like a preteen girl at a Hannah Montana concert. We went ahead and made the investment, which ended up working out in our favor. But even when our return came in, she never had the same level of excitement she had when she first found out about the idea. By then, she'd moved on to the next thing.

- **Love finding your next adventure.** We know a Risk Taker who is investing in a Vietnamese coffee farm. He doesn't know anything about coffee production, he's never seen the land he's buying, and he doesn't care. For Risk Takers, no idea is too out there, no risk too big. Their sense of adventure takes over, and they want in.

- **Listen to your gut.** More than conventional wisdom, more than financial experts, a Risk Taker trusts her intuition. If a deal doesn't feel right, she won't do it. But if something strikes her, she's on it.

- **Aren't afraid to make decisions.** Risk Takers don't dink around when it comes to money. They make a decision and make it fast. That can be a real plus when there are important financial decisions on the line. When Risk Takers come into our offices, they usually know what their financial goals are and have a pretty good sense of how to reach them. They sometimes need our help rearranging their finances to make their risks possible, but they rarely need our input on whether or not to take those risks.

The Risk Taker has the obvious challenge of possibly losing everything in one deal that goes south. That's why it's essential that both partners believe in the next great deal. If the Risk Taker forges ahead without his partner's consent, he's committing financial infidelity. But there are other challenges that the Risk Taker might think about. If you're a Risk Taker, you need to be aware that you can be:

- **Vulnerable.** Risk Takers are often the victims of cons. We've met with all kinds of Risk Takers who come to us—sometimes without their partner's knowledge—hoping we can help them recover from a huge mistake. When the Risk Taker is young, there's plenty of time to recover. But too often we meet with retirees who have been the victims of scams. They got pulled into some fake reverse mortgage deal or invested a chunk of their savings in a sham venture, and they are devastated. The thrill of the deal and the desire for wealth can make for a toxic combination in the Risk Taker. Because this kind of loss can be such a blow, the Risk Taker might try to hide the loss from his partner by making more high-risk deals, shifting money around, even gambling in an effort to recoup the lost money.

- **Blinded by possibility.** That look I mentioned in Bethany's eyes? That look scares me. And it should scare a Risk Taker too. When a Risk Taker gets that look, reason has left the building. And with it go concern for other people's feelings, attention to detail, and long-range planning. In their place? The hiding and secrecy of financial infidelity.

- **Easily resented.** Even if a Risk Taker is in a relationship with another Risk Taker, the quick decisions, the leveraging of assets, can end with two people who don't like each other very much. When a decision pays off, everyone's happy, but all it takes is one bum deal to create a rift of resentment. That resentment can infect the relationship to the point that there is a complete absence of financial communication. And when that's missing, there is almost certainly financial infidelity. The Risk Taker might start being secretive about deals. His partner might set up private accounts to protect some of their money. All that hiding and sneaking around will eventually corrode the relationship beyond repair.

- **Impatient.** Risk Takers' decisiveness can cause them to lose patience with people who don't sign on to their big ideas as quickly as they'd like. Risk Takers don't know why other people can't see what they see, understand what they understand. They can even develop an inflated view of their own judgment, thinking other people aren't as smart or savvy as they are. Risk Takers often commit financial infidelity because of this impatience. They make decisions without consulting the people those decisions impact most—their partners. That might not feel like intentional secrecy to Risk Takers, but noncommunication is noncommunication, no matter what the motivation.

- **Insensitive.** Needless to say, that impatience can also lead to a disregard for other people's feelings. If the Risk Taker's partner gets nervous about the Risk Taker's behavior, the Risk Taker will often ignore those feelings and do what she wants to do anyway. Risk Takers hate feeling hemmed in by other people, so rather than work for compromise, they charge ahead and deal with the relational fallout later. And when the Risk Taker's partner isn't on board with the decision, there is always relational fallout. By making decisions that impact his partner with little to no consideration for her fears or concerns, the Risk Taker is essentially controlling his partner's financial future.

The Security Seeker

Carolyn is retired. Her husband was in banking, so they set up a healthy retirement fund early in their marriage and are now living very comfortably. Carolyn also inherited a lot of money when her favorite aunt died, along with several stocks in an energy company that supplies power for several states. In other words, Carolyn has plenty of money. But she worries about her health. She wonders if she's going to be OK if her husband dies before she does. She checks her stocks every morning and again every night to see how the market is doing. She wonders if she needs to sell off a few shares and put that money in a CD.

Carolyn thinks she and her husband need better life and health insurance plans. They can afford to increase their premiums, and she's been pressuring him to do that for months. He thinks they're fine as they are, but Carolyn's not sure. She doesn't want to lose their home if one of them gets sick and needs long-term care. She wants to make sure they'll have enough money to pay for a good nursing home if that's what's needed. So she's started putting a little extra money into low-risk investments. She hasn't told her husband, but she's certain it's the right decision. That secrecy is an act of financial infidelity.

Scott is the Security Seeker in a Risk Taker's world. We have built our business from scratch and there have been times—plenty of them—when we weren't sure what the future would look like. Would we end up with a thriving business or find ourselves losing everything and starting over? I love that tension,

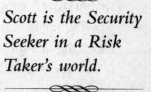

Scott is the Security Seeker in a Risk Taker's world.

but for Scott, it's excruciating. He would just as soon be an employee, have a regular paycheck every month, and know that his retirement account is safe and sound. There are times when I'm talking about some new venture we ought to consider to build the business and Scott just ducks out of the conversation. The anxiety is too much.

Scott is a typical Security Seeker. He wants to know our house will be paid off. He wants to make sure our retirement is sufficient. He wants to make sure our future is settled and safe. Security Seekers are looking for just that—security. They don't care if they have a lavish retirement; they just want to know they won't be living on the streets. They don't care if they have the nicest house in town; they just want one they can pay for. These are the people who put a little money into stocks, call their brokers every morning, and panic if there's a 5 percent drop in the market. We know one couple in which both partners are Security Seekers. They found a great house that was a little out of their price range, but they worked out an interest-only loan that gave them payments they could afford. They refinanced a year later because they just couldn't stand the tension of not building equity and not knowing if some drastic turn of events would prevent them from paying off their mortgage.

If simply reading the term *interest-only loan* makes you nervous, you're probably a Security Seeker. And if that's the case, you are:

- **An investigator.** Remember our friend with the Vietnamese coffee farm? The whole idea freaks Scott out. A Security Seeker would never invest in a piece of property he'd never seen. In fact, a Security Seeker wouldn't just need to see the property; he'd need to have the soil tested for toxicity, look into all the zoning restrictions within a three-mile area, find out where the schools are, and get a detailed prospectus from the developer and a résumé from every other investor.

- **Trustworthy.** Security Seekers rarely put their futures on the line. That means they aren't likely to gamble away their retirement or tap into the college fund to join a multilevel marketing company. Security Seekers would rather have a low return on their investment than risk losing the investment altogether.

- **Willing to sacrifice.** A Security Seeker would rather do without today than do without tomorrow. Even though Scott is also a Spender, his Security Seeker side means he doesn't spend until he's contributed to our retirement, our life insurance, and all the other investments he's set up to make sure our future is taken care of. And if that means he has to take on new clients to bring in extra income for spending, that's OK with him. He'd rather put in the extra time than scrimp on our savings.

- **Prepared for anything.** Security Seekers are never caught without a plan. If one partner gets sick and can't work, the Security Seeker has it covered through disability insurance. If the car gets hit or the laptop stolen, the Security Seeker has the homeowners' and car insurance to take care of it. The Security Seeker rarely ends up in a financial crisis (at least not a real crisis—that 5 percent stock market dip can feel like a crisis to the Security Seeker), which means the rest of the family can rest a little easier.

The Security Seeker's challenges are a bit like those of the Saver— the joy stealing, the fixation on money, the temptation to keep money secrets (all of which can lead to financial infidelity). But Scott is an example of a Security Seeker who still loves to spend—as long as it doesn't take away from his long-range goals. So while there is a bit of overlap between the traits of a Saver and those of a Security Seeker, there are also challenges that are unique to the Security Seeker. If you're a Security Seeker, you need to be aware that you can:

- **Be overly negative.** As a Security Seeker, my first response to most money questions is no. Bethany deals with this a lot from me whenever we talk about our long-term planning. She's a Risk Taker, so she often gets ideas about how a little bit of risk could pay off big. But my tendency is to pass on the risk without even hearing more about it, because I honestly don't want to know. Just thinking about risk makes me nervous, so I try to avoid that feeling by shutting off the conversation as quickly as possible. When Security Seekers shut out their partners, they leave room for all kinds of financial secrets—their own, and their partner's. The Security Seeker can become controlling, using his veto power to keep his partner from exploring her own financial dreams.

- **Get stuck in a research rut.** We call this tendency paralysis by analysis. In other words, Security Seekers can get so caught up in making sure an opportunity is foolproof that they never act. While that careful investigation can be helpful and often keeps Security Seekers from falling into bad investments, it can also cause them to miss out on truly great opportunities. Again, this challenge can quickly become controlling behavior. The Security Seeker might demand to be the one to determine where the couple invests their money, shutting his partner out of their financial decisions altogether and leading him into financial infidelity.

- **Stifle creativity.** This challenge doesn't just impact other
  people in the Security Seeker's life, it impacts the Security
  Seeker too. Over time, that need for security can become
  so all-consuming that she stops looking at the possibilities
  of the future and sticks with the certainties—and that can
  be a very subtle form of control. Life demands some flex-
  ibility, some room for discovery and changes of course. But
  when one partner shuts out possibilities, she has effectively
  eliminated any choice the other person has for his future.

The Flyer

Emily is a Flyer. She's an actress, an artist, a writer, a dreamer. She's
never been very good at keeping track of her money, so she actually
likes using a credit card so she can just pay for everything with one
check. Before she got married, Emily just paid the minimum balance on her monthly bill and felt good about keeping on top of her
payments. Once she got married, her husband showed her just how
much interest she was paying on her credit card. Emily was stunned.
She never knew how that all worked, and didn't really care. But when
someone added up the numbers for her, it was pretty ugly. She didn't
like so much of her money going to the credit card company. So her
husband helped her make a plan for paying down her debt. Now she's
debt free and it doesn't matter to her one bit. Debt, no debt. No big
deal. She's glad she's not losing money anymore, but as long as her
husband is willing to take care of all that, she's fine.

The Flyer is perhaps the most unusual money personality in that
the outlook has very little to do with money. Flyers don't think about
money—at all. They're not anxious about it, they're not consumed by
it, they have absolutely no emotional response to money. If you're a
Flyer, someone else probably bought this book for you—maybe you

Flyers don't think about money—at all.

didn't even know there was a whole section in the bookstore about finances. But the Flyer is a money personality because unless the Flyer has gone off to some isolated island and formed an alternative government that works strictly on a barter system (and that's totally something a Flyer would do), even the Flyer has to deal with money now and then.

We call this money personality the Flyer because these are the people who fly by the seat of their pants. They live paycheck to paycheck and probably don't really know how much has been taken out of that paycheck for taxes. They don't get excited about saving, they don't get excited about spending. They simply use money as a means to creating the lives they want.

Even Flyers have one of the other money personalities as well. A Flyer who has a secondary Saver money personality will dump all their change in a jar but never do anything with it. A Flyer who has a secondary Spender money personality will never let that change hit the jar— even if he's only got a buck, the Flyer/Spender will spend it, probably on coffee with a friend. A Flyer who has a secondary Risk Taker money personality will find out there's a gallery space available in a terrible neighborhood and jump on it, even if she has no idea if she can afford it. And a Flyer who has a secondary Security Seeker money personality will either live in his parents' basement for as long as possible, or find another Security Seeker who will handle all the money issues.

If you're a Flyer, you are also:

- **Basically content with your life.** A Flyer might be dirt poor and living in an Airstream out by the highway, but he doesn't care. As long as a Flyer is making his own choices, he's happy.

- **Big on relationships.** For Flyers, relationships and connections with other people are crucial. Flyers will often put relationships above a financial task. That's good news for anyone in a relationship with a Flyer. They are willing to participate in financial conversations if they matter to the other person.

- **Happy to let someone else take care of your finances.** This can be a big plus in relationships, especially if the other partner has one of the other money personalities. The Flyer won't criticize the Saver's efforts to cut back. She won't jump on the Spender about wasting money. She won't get anxious around the Risk Taker or impatient with the Security Seeker. The Flyer is just glad someone else is paying attention to all that money stuff.

- **Not motivated by money.** Most Flyers end up living exactly the lives they want to live because they make choices based on what they want, not what will make them the most money, so they rarely end up in careers they hate (unless someone has convinced them to take that job for the sake of the relationship).

Flyers are great people to be with. But this money personality has its challenges just like the others. If you're not a Flyer, you can probably guess what they are because just reading about the Flyer has made you nervous. But Flyers are pretty blind to these challenges because, again, they don't think about money and therefore don't think about how their money personality impacts them. But it does. If you're a Flyer, you need to be aware that you can be:

- **Reactionary.** Flyers don't think about money, but money is a necessary part of life. So sooner or later, even Flyers have to pay attention to their bills or their looming retirement. It usually takes a dramatic wake-up call of some kind—an illness, a new baby, a sixty-fifth birthday—to get the Flyer to start thinking about money. And when they do, they often make financial decisions based on fear, not good advice. That lack of planning can lead them into deep debt, debt they pass on to their partners.

- **Lacking in the skills needed to solve your financial problems.** As we've said, it rarely occurs to a Flyer to seek help from a financial planner. So when money problems come up, the Flyer tries to handle it himself, but because he doesn't care about money, he doesn't have any idea how finances work. Interest? Consolidation? Refinancing? These concepts aren't on his radar. So he tries to solve the problem the only way he knows how—by ignoring it and hoping it will go away. That kind of noncommunication and lack of involvement is a big foothold for financial infidelity. But ignoring debt doesn't make it go away. Instead, this head-in-the-sand approach is what leads to people to having their cars repossessed or their houses foreclosed. The person in a relationship with a Flyer becomes the victim of the Flyer's poor planning.

- **Disorganized.** Flyers aren't always disorganized people in the general sense, but when it comes to money, they are all over the place. We've asked Flyers to bring in tax returns, and they have no idea where something like that might be. Some of them don't even remember if they filed taxes or what their taxable income is. We know a Flyer who works from home. Every year, her husband asks her to hang on to her receipts for any business-related expenses. And every year at tax time, she has no idea where she put them. She isn't trying to be irritating; she just didn't make a plan for where to put her receipts and how to keep track of her expenses. This disorganization can lead the Flyer's partner to feel like he has no choice but to exert control over the Flyer's financial life, possibly hiding money and keeping other financial secrets in an effort to keep the family ship from sinking. In other words, the Flyer's behavior contributes to all kinds of financial infidelity, even when she is seemingly uninvolved in the finances.

- **Unresponsible.** Anyone who isn't a Flyer might think Flyers are irresponsible. But really, they are *un*responsible. Irresponsibility suggests a deliberate lack of maturity. But Flyers aren't trying to be lazy or inattentive. They genuinely don't think about money issues, so they don't actively participate in their own financial lives. They leave themselves open to the control of their partners. And allowing yourself to be controlled is as much a part of financial infidelity as doing the controlling.

SOMETHING TO TALK ABOUT

Talk about your money personalities with your partner. What are some of the positive things your partner's money personality brings to your relationship?

Chapter Three

When Money Personalities Collide

*I*n our experience dealing with thousands of clients, we've seen every possible combination of money personalities. We've seen couples at the brink of divorce because their money personalities clashed so severely. We've seen couples with such astonishingly bad communication that we wonder how they managed to show up at our office at the same time. But we've seen some of these same couples learn to understand each other, forgive each other, and move into their future with a new sense of how to overcome financial infidelity and reach their financial goals.

We're going to tell you some horror stories in this chapter, but we're also going to tell you about those couples who have survived financial infidelity and turned their marriages around. The key to those turnarounds is communication. And real communication starts with understanding each other.

> *We've seen couples at the brink of divorce because their money personalities clashed so severely.*

Now that you and your partner have figured out your money personalities, you're going to look at how those personalities interact.

Obviously we could use the rest of this book to cover all the various combinations of primary and secondary money personalities. But for the sake of getting to the point, we're going to break down the five most common conflicts between money personalities and show you how to deal with them.[1] While not every personality combination is covered, the principles for overcoming conflict are the same. Before you get started, there are a few thoughts we want you to keep in mind:

- Because each money personality has its own strengths and challenges, each combination of money personalities leads to a different kind of financial infidelity issue. You'll need to keep in mind the descriptions you just read as you look over these combinations. Look for the ways the strengths and challenges of each money personality contribute to the conflicts described in this chapter. And look for the ways those strengths can also help two money personalities gel into a great partnership.

- Our money personalities shape our assumptions and expectations about money. Savers expect other people to want to save too. Spenders assume everyone gets the same thrill from spending that they do. When those types of expectations aren't met, our money personalities can drive us to take extreme action to reduce our own anxieties. As you look at the conflicts that happen in your relationship, be aware of the assumptions you tend to make. Do your best to be honest about the expectations you have and how those impact your financial relationship.

- We can't stress this enough: you can't change a person's money personality, including your own. But money personalities—

like every other part of who we are—can mature. We can all become less selfish and more considerate. None of the conflicts you'll read about in this chapter could have been resolved without both partners being willing to grow.

Combination #1:
The Spender and the Saver

The Real-Life Story

Kim and Ed had been married for about ten years when they came in to see us. Kim was the Spender. She had grown up very poor; her parents were Christian missionaries, so everything they had came from other people. Ed was the Saver who grew up in a relatively wealthy family. He had a great job and made plenty of money, so Kim decided to stay home with the kids.

We asked them what was going on, and they spilled it. Kim said that because they live in a nice house and Ed has a good job, she should be able to spend what she wants. Ed said he did the finances for the family and he saw all this money flying out of their pockets every month.

In Kim's mind, she deserves to spend whatever she wants. Since she grew up with nothing, she feels like she should be able to have everything now. And she wants her kids to have everything too. She feels a deep resentment when Ed tries to take that freedom away from her. By the time they came to see us, Kim had started hiding her spending from Ed, so not only was she spending money while knowing it bothered him, she was lying about it. There was some intense financial infidelity in this relationship, and Kim wasn't about to make a change.

In Ed's mind, Kim was spending money he was working hard to earn. He resented her spending, not only because he thought it was excessive, but because he felt like it was *his* money. He had a whole set of expectations about *how* his money should be spent, and it bore no resemblance to how Kim was spending it.

We've said this plenty of times already, and we'll keep saying it: Kim and Ed's problems had nothing to do with money. She hadn't spent them into bankruptcy. No, they were at odds because they had stopped communicating, stopped trusting each other, stopped acting like partners. Instead, they were stuck in a cycle of lying and hiding and controlling that meant their relationship was in much bigger trouble than their checkbook.

The Problem

When couples meet, they are attracted to their differences. The Spender sees the Saver as someone who will be responsible, who will help her take good care of her money. The Saver loves the lavish gifts, the attention, the spoiling he gets from the Spender. Then they get married and the differences they loved so much become intolerable. He wants her to stop wasting money; she wants him to stop controlling her. He's afraid she's going to drive them into debt; she's afraid he's going to take all the fun out of life.

This combination is a tough one because it involves a couple's day-to-day lives. The Saver wants to make dinner at home; the Spender wants to go out. The Spender gets herself a nice bathrobe, and the Saver resents it every morning when he sees it hanging on the hook. The Saver buys single-ply toilet paper, and the Spender gets literally and figuratively chafed every time she uses it. These might sound like petty examples, but if this is your combination, you know they are just scratching the surface. Remember Holly, the woman who was still ticked off that her husband bought that $35 coffee mug? That's this couple.

She's a Saver, he's a Spender, and every little purchase creates tension. This combination can quickly degenerate into all kinds of shaming and controlling behavior, like the kind we saw in Ed and Kim's relationship. The Saver can try to clamp down on the Spender, which leaves the Spender feeling like a child who can't be trusted with money. Or the Spender belittles the Saver's efforts by calling him petty or cheap. It can even run into other parts of the relationship. If the Spender comes home from Target with gifts for

She's a Saver, he's a Spender, and every little purchase creates tension.

the kids and the Saver makes a comment, the Spender can feel like her partner is putting limits on how she shows love to her children. The Saver can feel like his partner is spoiling the kids. The whole thing becomes a mess of accusations and hurt feelings.

The Solution

The only way any couple can work through the financial conflicts is to acknowledge that the other person's money personality is valid. There is no right money personality, no wrong money personality. They are just different. Once couples understand those differences and start respecting what the other person brings to the partnership, they can start moving out of their patterns of financial infidelity.

For the Spender and the Saver, open communication is crucial. Here's how they can put an end to financial infidelity:

- **Talk about the tension.** Every couple can benefit from talking about the tension in their financial relationship. But for this combination in particular, communication is essential. These two money personalities are so very different from one another that without honest conversation, it's almost impossible for these two to understand each other. We asked Kim to explain to Ed why she liked spending money. He had never really considered her background and what it must have been like to live on so little. Then we had Ed talk about his fears of losing everything he was working for. Kim hadn't ever heard him talk about fear, and as she listened, she started to see that he wasn't mad, he was afraid.

- **Be clear about their needs.** Because the Spender and the Saver have such different needs, it's essential that they articulate those needs clearly. Kim needed to feel a sense of freedom, and Ed had to acknowledge that and maybe let go of—or at least not always act on—his fears of losing everything. Ed needed to trust that there would be enough money available for the family to deal with emergencies. Kim had to be willing to limit herself a bit for his sake.

- **Create a true partnership.** The Saver and Spender combination can make it tough for couples to see themselves as partners. Again, their opposing ideas about money can easily lead to both partners feeling like they are in a constant battle with the other person's money personality, so developing a sense of partnership is an absolutely essential part of repairing this relationship. We helped Kim and Ed get there by showing Kim their family budget, something Ed had never done. We sat down with both of them while Ed explained every line item to her. "Here's what we pay on the house every month, here's our life insurance payment, here's what we put into the kids' college savings, here's what I like to have in our checking account in case some emergency comes up." Ed showed her that "his" money was funding "their" life together, something neither of them had really thought about before. They began to see that they had a kind of family business together, and that conversation helped both of them see Kim as a partner in that business. This simple shift in perspective allowed them to work together in ways they didn't think possible.

- **Set limits—together.** Once they had a better understanding of their budget, Ed and Kim worked together to figure out what kind of freedom Kim could have with her spending. Ed said, "I'm not saying you can never spend anything, but I want to make sure we can pay for the necessities. I want to make sure that if the car breaks down we can take care of it, that if I lose my job tomorrow we'll be OK." Kim could say, "OK, when I look at this, it seems like we have about $500 every month that's not dedicated to something else. It seems like it works for us if I stick to a $500 limit on my spending." This wasn't an allowance Ed deemed appropriate for his little Kimmy; this was an amount they agreed they could both live with. Ed had the safety net he needed; Kim had the freedom she needed.

- **Determine their spending priorities.** Working together also allowed Ed and Kim to talk about what Kim would spend that money on. Since she was no longer spending out of frustration and spite, she and Ed made some decisions about purchases that would be fun for the whole family—vacations, a karaoke machine, new bikes.

Combination #2:
The Spender and the Security Seeker

The Real-Life Story

Marc and Sarah had been married for seven years, and they had been fighting about money for six and a half of them. This is Sarah's second marriage. She came into her marriage to Marc with significant debt from her first marriage. But as a Spender, Sarah thought everyone had a lot of debt; it's just what happens when you spend money.

Marc had been on his own for about ten years by the time he and Sarah got married. He had a solid job with great potential and had worked hard to build up good credit, put some money into a retirement account, and started saving for a house. As a Security Seeker, he wanted to make sure all his hard work would pay off later and that he—and his future family—would be protected.

At first Sarah loved how stable Marc was, how careful he was about money. She loved that he was ready to buy a house for them right away. And Marc loved how classy Sarah was, how well she fit in with his wealthier coworkers. Their first Christmas together, Sarah and Marc hosted a beautiful Christmas party for their families and friends. Sarah pulled out all the stops—the house looked gorgeous, the food was perfect, and she had picked out meaningful gifts for everyone who came.

But the lovefest came to a sudden stop around mid-January when the bills rolled in. When Marc saw how much Sarah had spent on the party, he was furious. And Sarah? She was just confused. Didn't Marc know what it cost to throw a great party? Did he think all those gifts came from the dollar store? She couldn't understand how he could claim ignorance and then get mad at her.

This pattern of Sarah spending and Marc fretting had gone on for most of their married life. Sarah rarely went a day without buying something, even if it was just a triple mocha for her drive to work and a salad over her lunch hour. And Marc rarely went a day without reminding Sarah of how much she was spending.

Sarah was so tired of Marc's nagging and nitpicking that she'd just stopped telling him about most of her purchases. She knew he was going to see the bill and freak out, but she'd rather deal with a couple of rough days than have to explain every purchase she made.

Marc was tired too. He was tired of Sarah ringing up hundreds, sometimes thousands of dollars on the credit card each month even when he'd asked her not to. He was tired of coming home to shopping bags or finding a new pair of shoes in Sarah's closet or a new lamp on the end table that she never mentioned buying. He was tired of working ten-hour days trying to have some kind of savings for the future only to see that money turn into lattes and designer handbags. He'd gotten so fed up that he secretly upped their retirement savings just to make sure Sarah couldn't spend everything they had before they got there.

Marc and Sarah ended up in a state of financial infidelity because neither of them could see that the other person had a genuine need for their finances to work a certain way. And until they started talking to each other about those needs, they would keep cheating on each other.

The Problem

The main point of contention for these two is the security part of their financial picture. The Spender wants to spend now, and the Security Seeker wants to shove the money under the mattress for later. The Spender is thinking about today, and the Security Seeker is thinking about tomorrow.

The Spender is thinking about today, and the Security Seeker is thinking about tomorrow.

The Security Seeker isn't necessarily opposed to spending—unless that spending eats away at the couple's retirement account or life insurance policy or college fund or mortgage payments. As long as those investments are solid and sound, the Security Seeker is a happy camper.

The Spender isn't necessarily opposed to planning ahead—unless all that planning means the family finances are tied up in stocks and investments that no one can touch for thirty years. The Spender likes having actual cash on hand. Sure the future is important, but so is the present. In Spenderland, life is meant to be lived today.

Both of these money personalities are motivated by money, but for very different reasons. And that's where the tension comes from. For the Spender, money is a tool for living life to the fullest, so he wants to have enough money to do everything he wants to do. The Security Seeker, however, is focused on security, on the certainty that everything will be OK. The Spender doesn't just spend money; he spends little bits of the Security Seeker's safety net. And that creates tremendous anxiety in the Security Seeker.

So the Security Seeker looks for ways to control the spending, to get rid of that anxiety. She might try to give the Spender an allowance—which the Spender is bound to both resent and blow through—or hide some money in a secret account so she knows she's got something the Spender can't touch. Ironically, the Spender may very well have the exact same response, hiding money to make sure he has some source of cash the Security Seeker won't try to claim. Regardless of why it's done, this kind of hiding is blatant financial infidelity.

The Solution

This is a couple that needs to learn how to compromise. More than just about any other pairing, these two can end up with such completely different goals that they are basically living separate lives. The Spender wants to have fun, the Security Seeker wants to feel safe, and those goals crash into each other with nearly every decision they make.

Here's what the Spender and Security Seeker can do:

- **Recognize the Security Seeker's fear.** Marc had to be honest about his fears: Fears that if something happened to him, Sarah wouldn't have enough money. Fears that they would end up with nothing to show for their decades of hard work. Fears that if he lost his job, they wouldn't have any money to fall back on. And Sarah needed to recognize that these fears were real. These things can and do happen to lots of people. Marc wasn't being paranoid or controlling when he planned for the worst. He was taking care of the people he loved. That's what Security Seekers do. When Sarah started to see Marc's behavior as his way of caring for her, she found it much easier to accept his financial decisions.

- **Understand the Spender's motivation.** For Sarah, spending was a way of creating the life she'd always wanted, one filled with parties and friends and a beautiful house and great clothes. But it's the life itself that matters to her—all of that stuff is just the window dressing. Sarah had to tell Marc that she spends money because it makes her feel good about her marriage, her home, her work. Money was part of the image she had of what a grown-up life looks like. Marc had to realize that just because he doesn't think about money in those terms, doesn't mean Sarah is irresponsible. In fact, Marc often reaps the benefits of Sarah's generosity and efforts to create a comfortable life for them. When he started to notice the care she put into choosing cushy bath towels or fresh flowers for the living room, he gained a new respect for the work behind their lovely life together. When he thought about the vacations she'd arranged for them and the concerts and events they'd gone to, he saw that she had given him incredible experiences he never would have considered on his own.

- **Commit to real change.** If this marriage was going to survive, Sarah needed to recognize that her spending was hurting her husband in real ways. His anger toward her was a visceral reaction to his internal anxiety and fear. She had to decide if she wanted to contribute to his anxiety or help calm it. And if she was invested in making their relationship work, she only had one choice. She had to agree to a budgeted spending amount and stick to it. And she had to stop hiding and lying about her spending. Marc would never be able to trust her if she continued to spend behind his back; for a Security Seeker, this kind of financial infidelity pushes all of their paranoia buttons and makes them work even harder to prevent financial ruin. For his part, Marc had to look at the ways he might have been overreacting to his anxiety and how to become a bit more realistic about the risks they faced. He realized he probably didn't need the two million dollar life insurance plan, that he could pull it back to one million and leave a little more cash in the daily reserves. He also needed to give Sarah some freedom to spend within the limits they worked out together, then trust her to live within those limits without watching her every purchase. Letting go of some control is incredibly difficult for a Security Seeker, but it's a step Marc had to make if he was going to make this relationship work.

- **Notice and encourage your partner.** When we talk with couples like Marc and Sarah, our hope is that they get to the point where the Spender can see all the ways the Security Seeker has taken care of the family. We want the Spender to notice the work that's gone into providing for the future—because it can be a lot of work. And we want the Security Seeker to see all the good the Spender brings into the relationship—the fun, the joy, the memories. When these two money personalities back up, let go of their fears a little, and start working together, they can create a fantastic partnership.

Combination #3:
The Saver and the Risk Taker

The Real-Life Story

Early on in their marriage, Steve and Mimi started a company. Steve, the Risk Taker, had a great idea. Mimi, the Saver, was a big help in getting that dream off the ground. They spent years building their company, and it was a huge success. They were making great money, driving hot cars, living in a gorgeous house. And if they had just stayed the course, they would have been fine.

But Risk Takers rarely stay the course. Steve had more big dreams and was ready to make those a reality too. He wanted to be a national player in the business world, so he decided the fastest way to get there was to leverage his biggest asset, their company. The problem is, he didn't talk to Mimi about it. He just dove in, finding investors and signing up a few friends, promising them a huge return on their investment.

Mimi had been a kind of silent partner in the company. She worked from home, taking care of their kids and doing the accounting. She knew every dime that came in and every dime that went out. She was proud of what they'd built together, but she was also totally content to ride their success calmly into the future.

But that's not what happened. Instead, the economy took a dive, and Steve lost everything. The new business tanked before it got off the ground. Steve owed a bunch of people a bunch of money. And the only way to pay it back was to sell off the original business. If Steve had been willing to stay where he was, they could have weathered the slump. Instead, he took a risk and paid for it with his friends, his life's work, and his reputation.

When they came to us, Mimi had already made it clear that she felt completely betrayed. She said, "Steve got so caught up in his ego that he didn't care what I thought or what I wanted. This was our business and I have worked so hard to build it with him, but that counts for nothing with him!" Steve felt terrible, but he also admitted he didn't tell Mimi about leveraging the company because he knew she'd object.

> *His financial infidelity had come back to bite him in a big way.*

His financial infidelity had come back to bite him in a big way.

The Problem

We could write a whole book about this relationship alone. It can be a complex, confusing coupling. The Risk Taker is willing to put every egg in one basket, while the Saver would like to keep those eggs out of baskets altogether. In other words, the Risk Taker has no problem taking everything the Saver holds dear and throwing it into some huge make-or-break deal. That tendency, of course, taps into the Saver's deepest financial fear—that all her money will be gone. At the same time, the Saver's tendency to hoard money and not spend unless it's absolutely necessary taps into the Risk Taker's deepest financial fear—that he will be controlled by someone else's decisions.

What makes this a bit more complicated than some of the other money personality pairs is that the Risk Taker isn't necessarily opposed to saving money. Many Risk Takers are very savvy about finances. They know they have to tighten the budget if they want to have enough available to make that big investment down the road. We see this in Risk Takers who want to get into real estate, for example, and are willing to drive old cars, live in dingy apartments, and wear secondhand clothes in order to save enough money to buy their first rental property.

And Savers aren't necessarily opposed to taking risks. Remember, Savers have an internal list of financial priorities—things they are willing to spend money on and things they aren't. We know Savers who won't shop anywhere but discount stores but who are willing to invest a good chunk of money in an opportunity like buying an apartment complex in Thailand.

But the combination of these two money personalities can turn combustible when the Saver and the Risk Taker stop talking about these nuances of their money personalities and instead make assumptions about each other. Because when the Saver assumes the Risk Taker is out to ruin them, that relationship is dying. And when the Risk Taker assumes the Saver is trying to kill her dreams, that relationship is dying. The killer is financial infidelity.

In Steve and Mimi's case, that infidelity took the form of a major secret. Steve didn't set out to hide his deal from Mimi—it just didn't occur to him to talk to her about it. But really, what's the difference? In a true partnership, it shouldn't occur to one person *not* to talk to the other about a big financial decision. If Steve valued Mimi's input, if he respected their relationship—both as business partners and husband and wife—he would have talked to her about this decision before making it.

Mimi plays a role here as well. Hers might not be as obvious as Steve's, but one of the reasons Steve gave for not talking to Mimi about this idea is that he knew she'd be against it. Somewhere along the line, Mimi made it clear that Steve's dreams and vision for their life together wasn't as important as their money. She has sent off a vibe of inflexibility and iron-fisted control over the finances. And that kind of control is financial infidelity too.

The Solution

Steve and Mimi created a great partnership when they started their business. They knew each other's strengths and figured out how to work together. They had lost that respect and collaborative spirit. But with time and grace, we think they can regain it.

Here's what the Saver and the Risk Taker can do:

- **Forgive, forgive, forgive.** Naturally, forgiveness is essential in all of these combinations, but this pairing in particular can create the kind of resentment that sucks the life out of relationships. The resentment a Saver can feel toward a Risk Taker creates an atmosphere in which the Risk Taker has to bear complete responsibility for everything that goes wrong in the Saver's life. It becomes a relationship filled with "If only you hadn't . . ." and, "You never should have . . ." And no relationship can last under that kind of blame. So we knew Steve and Mimi weren't going to get past this devastation without some real forgiveness and grace. Steve had to look Mimi in the eye and tell her he was sorry for making such a huge decision without her. He needed to heal the broken partnership. And Mimi needed to let go of her anger and resentment so she didn't hold this over his head for the rest of their lives.

- **Rebuild trust.** Mimi needed to decide whether or not she was willing to move forward and rebuild a life with Steve. She needed to decide if she could trust him again. Trust is a huge issue for Risk Takers. They need to know that their partners believe in them and their dreams. But when that trust has been abused or broken, both partners have to make a genuine effort to recapture it. It's taking a lot of time and a lot of painful conversations, but Steve and Mimi are slowly recovering from this experience. They are working on rebuilding their lives and are committed to doing it together.

- **Learn to communicate.** Once Steve and Mimi made the choice to work this out, we helped them learn how to develop stronger communication about their finances. The Risk Taker is prone to making impulsive decisions without consulting anyone. As we've said, that's a kind of secrecy, and it simply can't occur if a relationship is going to survive. So Steve and Mimi decided that until they were back on their feet financially and emotionally, they wouldn't make any financial decisions without talking to each other. That's a hard promise for a Risk Taker to make—they hate being controlled. But Steve needed to see that there is a difference between respecting his partner and being controlled by her. Mimi needed to start thinking about how much decision-making power she was willing to give Steve without questioning him or being overly pessimistic. So they looked at their budget—which was pretty much nothing—and figured out what they could live with. Mimi had to trust Steve enough to let him risk a little of their meager income as they tried to rebuild a business. But they set clear expectations for how much he could risk and how they would create a safety net in case things fell apart again. These are the kinds of decisions a couple can only make when they are committed to healthy financial communication.

Combination #4:
The Saver and the Flyer

The Real-Life Story

Caitlin and Dan are one of those couples who bicker. A lot. They bicker about which movie to see, what to have for dinner, which way the toilet paper should go—over or under. The one thing they rarely argue about is money.

That's because Dan is a Saver and Caitlin is a Flyer. Dan makes the money decisions and Caitlin is happy to go along with whatever he says. When Dan and Caitlin were dating, Dan knew that Caitlin could be a little . . . inattentive to her finances, but he assumed she just didn't know much about money. It wasn't until they got married and he tried to have money conversations with her that he realized she was perfectly capable of handling her money. She just didn't want to. She gave Dan full control of the budget. "Just tell me what you need from me, and I'll do it," she told him. And that worked out just fine for everyone.

At least for a while. After their first child was born, Dan and Caitlin decided it would be great for Caitlin, a professional photographer, to work from home. Caitlin had no problem getting new clients, staying booked, and bringing in a fair amount of income. But she was terrible with her bookkeeping. She would book a wedding or a photo session and get her down payment from the client. But when she was finished with the project, she often forgot to send an invoice for her final payment. Dan, however, kept a running tally of Caitlin's clients in his head for just such occasions. So he'd periodically ask, "Honey, did you get paid for that wedding yet?" And Caitlin would inevitably say, "Um, I'm not sure."

Dan tried creating spreadsheets for Caitlin, tried making up a calendar for her to mark payment deadlines, he even tried taking over her billing himself. But Caitlin was just too disorganized to give him the right information and to keep everything straight.

Finally Dan got fed up. He told her, "Every time you get a new client, let me know. I will contact them about the money, and I will take care of it. You just can't keep being so lazy about this."

Caitlin was deeply offended by Dan's words. She wasn't lazy; she was just not interested in the business side of her business. She had tried to follow Dan's plans but she'd forget or run out of time and never get back to keeping her records up to date.

Dan was tired of taking care of everything. He was tired of being the only one who worried about money. He knew he could get obsessive about it, but if Caitlin wasn't going to help him with the finances, how could he help but obsess?

Caitlin got so fed up with Dan's nagging that she started telling him little lies to keep him at bay. So when he asked about an invoice, she'd tell him she'd sent it even though she'd completely forgotten about that client. When he asked for receipts, she gave him the few she could find and failed to mention that she'd misplaced even more of them. To her, these half truths helped keep some peace in their relationship. She felt bad about lying, but she figured it was better than having Dan stressed out about money all the time.

Dan had a few secrets of his own. When Caitlin was out on a shoot, he'd often dig around in her files to see if there were clients she hadn't told him about or receipts she hadn't turned in. A few times, he even sent out final invoices in Caitlin's name, just to make sure she got paid. He justified this sneaking around as an attempt to keep track of her income. If she couldn't—or wouldn't—do it, what choice did he have?

The Problem

Welcome to financial hell. With this couple, you've got one person who is totally committed to making sure the bills get paid, paying attention to the checking account so nothing bounces, and planning the budget down to the last detail. And then you've got someone who doesn't give a rip. The Flyer might not even notice there's tension here unless the Saver says something. But the Saver feels every brush-off, every careless purchase, every break in the budget. Savers take a lot of pride in creating a budget and living within their means. They work hard to pay off their credit cards

> *The Flyer might not even notice there's tension here unless the Saver says something.*

every month. They get excited about buying jeans for five bucks. So when the Flyer doesn't even notice that there is a budget or that credit cards have to be paid eventually or that five bucks is a great price for jeans, the Saver feels totally unappreciated.

From there, it's a short trip to resentment. The Saver starts to feel like the parent of an irresponsible child. We've heard Savers who are married to Flyers say things like, "I feel like I'm the only grown-up in this relationship!" That sense of being solely responsible for the finances can lead the Saver to start hiding money from the Flyer to make sure it stays safe, or to just leave the Flyer completely out of all the financial decisions. And that's financial infidelity.

The Flyer usually loves this setup, at least for a while. She gets all the benefits of a well-run household without doing any of the work. The bills get paid, the kids go off to college, retirement rolls around, and what do you know? There's money!

But when Savers move into resentment mode, they often try to set up some rules for the Flyer to follow. And that's when the Flyer develops some resentments of her own. Flyers might seem childish to the other money personalities, but they don't appreciate being treated like children. Flyers married to Savers will say things like, "He acts like he's in charge of me, like he gets to decide what I do, where I go, how I spend my money. It's driving me crazy!"

The Solution

The best news for anyone in a relationship with a Flyer is that ending financial infidelity and replacing it with healthy financial communication is really just a matter of engagement. Where other money personality combinations have to overcome what are often deeply divergent perspectives, the Flyer doesn't have a perspective on money. So in this case, the Saver only has to pull the Flyer from neutral to drive, not reverse to drive.

Here's what the Saver and the Flyer can do:

- **Have reasonable expectations.** The struggle for Caitlin and Dan had been that Dan was trying to get Caitlin to shift, not into drive, but into hyperspeed. His efforts to help her get her books in order were wonderful accounting tools, but Caitlin doesn't want to be an accountant. She wants to be a photographer. To heal this relationship, Dan needed to bring Caitlin on board in ways that were manageable for her. So instead of creating a plan and imposing it on her, Dan needed to sit down with Caitlin and find out what she was willing and able to do. How often could she collect her receipts and expenses? When did it make sense in her schedule to send out invoices? What would make it easier for her to remember to close out a project? And Caitlin needed to ask a little more of herself. If she was going to be a freelance photographer, she had to take at least a little responsibility for making that arrangement work. And if she couldn't, then she and Dan needed to look into other options for her work situation. Maybe she needed to "hire" Dan as her assistant. Maybe she could work for an agency that did all the booking and billing for her for a small fee. Whatever the options, Dan and Caitlin needed to be realistic about what they could—and would—do to make this work.

- **Start with a little involvement at a time.** Dan needed to pull back and recognize that Caitlin's money personality means she would never get the same thrill he does from keeping neat records. She will never have her first thought of the day be, *Oh good, I get to balance my books today.* Once he let go of his need to turn Caitlin into a Saver, he could engage her in a way that she could handle. He couldn't expect her to initiate financial conversations, but he could ask her to set aside forty-five minutes once a week for them to talk through her workload and update her books. And he needed to stop treating Caitlin like a child. He could ask for her help and input, but he had to accept that he would always be a lot more interested in this issue than she would. And he needed to quit snooping around. If he had questions for Caitlin, he needed to ask her. His secret searches were the kind of control and deceit that have no place in a healthy financial relationship.

- **Encourage the Saver's hard work.** Caitlin needed to do some repair work in this relationship too. She needed to start acknowledging and encouraging all the effort Dan put into keeping their finances humming. Dan had been careful about their spending, always making sure they had enough in the budget to pay the bills. He made sure they never accrued interest. He helped Caitlin find good deals on camera equipment and office supplies. Caitlin could do wonders for their relationship simply by noticing when Dan makes a sound financial decision. A statement like, "Dan, you have skills and an interest in this stuff I just don't have. And I really appreciate you using them to take care of our family," will make Dan feel like the money king. Caitlin also needed to stop lying to Dan. If she felt uncomfortable with the way he treated her, then she needed to step up and show him that she is responsible. Lying to him only confirmed that she couldn't be trusted with her own finances.

- **Be a true partner.** The Flyer's biggest challenge is staying invested in the financial relationship. When Flyers check out, they are paving the way for financial infidelity. Even if the Flyer's partner doesn't want to be controlling or secretive, the fact that the Flyer pays no attention to the finances means the other person *is* in control of the Flyer, and that's a situation that never turns out well. For this partnership to thrive, Caitlin needed to stop being passive and take at least a little responsibility for their financial life.

When Dan asks Caitlin for her input and her attention on some financial matter, she needs to be willing to put her money personality to rest for a bit and step up to the plate—because that's what partners do. Dan needs to try to include Caitlin in financial decisions, even when she doesn't seem all that interested. He needs to keep her in the loop.

Combination #5:
The Risk Taker and the Security Seeker

The Real-Life Story

Pete and Liz got married right out of college. They had very little income for the first few years and while it was kind of romantic, it could also be stressful. Some months they ate a lot of cereal. Some months they had to squeeze the budget even tighter just to pay the rent.

Pete was one of those people with big plans. He wanted to start a company, maybe a few companies. He liked dabbling in marketing and design and music and about twenty other things. He didn't mind not having money because he knew his day was coming.

Poverty made Liz nervous. Every month she worried they were going to lose their apartment. She wondered how they would ever afford to have kids—they could barely feed themselves. And she got a big knot in her stomach whenever she dared to think about having a house of their own. She just knew it wasn't going to happen.

But it did. Over the course of just ten years, Pete started three successful marketing businesses from scratch. For Pete, the businesses themselves weren't all that interesting. He liked the pursuit, the rush of getting something new off the ground. So he sold off each of his companies to pay for the next one.

Liz was glad they weren't living on Cheerios anymore, but every time Pete got some new idea in his head, she felt that familiar fear that this would be the one to break them. She got so tired of the stress Pete's ideas caused her that she started shutting him out when he told her about his latest passion. Pete didn't really care. He was happy to be unencumbered by Liz's opinions.

Pete decided he was tired of marketing and wanted to try a whole new enterprise: a restaurant. He was pretty vague with Liz about the details, hoping to keep her from mucking up his plans. The little she did know was enough to make her roll her eyes at the latest of Pete's big ideas. So he pressed on, and she checked out.

He found a building to lease, started getting all his permits in place, had all the wheels turning. And then the health inspector came by to look at the building. It was far from being up to code for a restaurant. As the inspector handed Pete his long list of problem areas, Pete felt his dream losing air. Fast.

He had leveraged most of the family assets to get this thing going. He'd bought equipment, he'd started remodeling. He was in deep. And there was no way he could get a big enough loan to pay for the renovations he needed. He'd already gotten a huge chunk that he'd be struggling to pay back.

When he talked to Liz that night, she was furious. She'd known something like this would happen and now it had. Pete had destroyed their finances.

The Problem

This is where Bethany and I clash. For the most part, Risk Takers and Security Seekers don't butt heads over the daily financial decisions. It's when we talk about the future that words fly and fingers point and fears come out.

Risk Takers and Security Seekers both want to invest for the future. But the Risk Taker wants to invest in land and Vietnamese coffee farms. Security Seekers like bonds and CDs. The Risk Taker is attracted to the potential for a high return; the Security Seeker is attracted to the guarantee that there will be something there in the future.

If each person in this couple could do their own thing, they'd be fine. But that's not much of a relationship. Yet when they try to make investment decisions together, one of them ends up frustrated. The Risk Taker feels stifled by the conservative Security Seeker. The Security Seeker feels terrified by the aggressive Risk Taker. Even when I know in my head that Bethany is making a smart investment, my gut has a

The Risk Taker feels stifled by the conservative Security Seeker.

very hard time. It gets to the point where I just don't want her to talk about it until it's all over.

One of the biggest issues we see in this combination is the I-told-you-so problem. And both of these types do it. If the Risk Taker makes it big despite the Security Seeker's concerns, it's so easy for the Risk Taker to hold that up as a reason to keep taking bigger and bigger risks. And if one of those risks bombs, it's so easy for the Security Seeker to use that bomb as a weapon whenever the Risk Taker brings up a new idea.

And that's when the financial infidelity starts. The Risk Taker simply quits talking about the investment opportunities he's pursuing. He makes unilateral decisions with no concern for the Security Seeker's very real need not to become destitute. The Security Seeker finds ways to pull money out of the Risk Taker's hands—tying it up in hidden investments, opening a secret bank account for emergencies, that kind of thing. There's a total lack of trust.

The Solution

Pete and Liz are like so many of the Security Seeker and Risk Taker combinations we meet. They have such incredibly different approaches to the future that unless they are totally committed to understanding each other and working together, they end up in devastating situations.

Here's what the Risk Taker and the Security Seeker can do:

- **Start talking. A lot.** Too often, couples with this combination of money personalities get stuck in their myopic worlds, unwilling or unable to see the other person's point of view. They tend to pull into themselves, shut out the other person, and live parallel lives that have no connection to each other. That's why we encourage these couples to start talking. Pete needs to keep Liz up-to-date on potential investments and current deals and ask for her input. And as hard as it can be, Liz needs to listen to these updates and give careful, thoughtful, nonreactive feedback. This kind of communication helps both of them get some basic needs met. Security Seekers need validation, so Liz needs to know that her fears and concerns matter to Pete, that he knows they are real and not just efforts to derail his dreams. The Risk Taker needs to know that his partner trusts him, so while Pete is content to make his own decisions, he feels a lot better about those decisions when he knows Liz believes in them too. This kind of open conversation can go a long way toward ending—and preventing—financial infidelity.

- **Learn to listen.** When Liz and Pete started talking, Pete found out that Liz had some great ideas for the restaurant, ideas that might have led him to make very different decisions along the way. And Liz discovered that Pete's intentions had always been to build a better life for their family. He sees his risky endeavors as a way to make a lot of money in a short amount of time, money he can use to pay for family vacations and the kids' college tuition. Once they started talking and paying attention to each other's needs, Liz and Pete were able to work together to repair their financial situation. Now they're talking about starting a coffee shop, a dream both of them are excited about. Scott and I have learned similar lessons through our experiences as this kind of couple. I've learned that I have to acknowledge Scott's fears when we're about to take some big financial risk. I have to listen, and I have to be willing to step away from a deal if he doesn't agree to it. And Scott has learned that he can trust me, that I won't just plunge us off the edge of some cliff.

- **Diversify.** If our whole future is tied up in some crazy, high-risk project, Scott's going to have an ulcer from all that stress. If it's all poured into CDs over the years, I'm going to get an ulcer from the frustration of it all. Couples like us and Pete and Liz can find a happy medium by diversifying investments. Pete and Liz settled on the coffee shop idea because it was a great outlet for Pete's entrepreneurial spirit but didn't involve the huge investment of capital that a restaurant did. As part of their reformed partnership, Pete and Liz also decided to put some money into a low-risk retirement fund. This helped Liz feel like they had something to fall back on if disaster struck again. It's this kind of compromise, developed out of honest communication, that keeps financial infidelity from infecting a relationship.

- **Practice grace.** This is a tough one for this combination. As we said, it's easy for these two to wield the past like a weapon. Liz had been using Pete's failure as a reason for tightening the budget and trying to control Pete's investments and spending. Every time she disagreed with a financial choice he made—whether it was the best way to consolidate their loans or how many gallons of milk to buy at a time—she let him know how little she trusted him. Sometimes she did it with overt criticism, sometimes with subtle looks of disgust. Pete didn't need to be reminded of what had happened. He had heaped more than enough shame on himself. At the same time, Pete found himself resenting Liz for being so uninvolved in the decision making. Sure, he'd been happy to move forward without her, but as he played the decision back in his mind, he realized he was angry at Liz for letting him plow ahead with such a big investment. Both of them had years' worth of pent-up resentment, anger, and frustration that they had to work through before they could truly create a new partnership. And the only way to start was to ask for—and offer—forgiveness. Liz apologized for checking out and leaving Pete to deal with the stressful decisions on his own. And Pete apologized for all the times he'd ignored Liz and made his own decisions. The grace they extended to one another is the foundation of their new life together.

Each of these couples experienced financial infidelity because their money personalities clashed in ways they never saw coming. Now that you and your partner know your money personalities and the ways they can create conflict in your financial relationship, you are in a great position to move out of financial infidelity and into a life of healthy financial communication.

In some ways, this has been the easy part—learning about yourselves and discovering why you feel the way you do about money, and why you and your partner conflict over money. But these discoveries are no good unless they help you figure out how to truly change the patterns of financial infidelity in your relationship. The next section of the book will help you identify these patterns and give you the tools you need to change them.

SOMETHING TO TALK ABOUT

Come up with three ways you can help your money personalities complement each other.

SECTION

2

Digging *Deeper*

Chapter Four

How Bad Is It? Finding Your Financial Infidelity Quotient

*O*K, before we go on, take a deep breath. You've just done some great work learning about money personalities and the part they play in financial infidelity. You've gained some new perspective on your partner and discovered why you butt heads when it comes to money. That's all great, but that's not all it takes to really get to the root of financial infidelity. To do that, you need to take an honest look at your past behavior and decide if you are going to keep going down the path you're on or if you're ready to stop, turn around, and move into a better future with your partner.

Behind every act of financial infidelity, there is a history of miscommunication and conflicts over money. You've discovered that those miscommunica-

> *Behind every act of financial infidelity, there is a history of miscommunication.*

tions and conflict are often the result of clashing money personalities. That's the *why* behind your financial issues: Why do you clash? Because you have very different perspectives about money. Now you need to think about *what* you do when those clashes occur, because it's in that decision—the *what*—that financial infidelity takes hold.

Earlier in the book we told you about a client whose husband had secretly given money to his ex-wife. His current wife was, understandably, livid. But his financial infidelity didn't start the day he handed a check to his ex. That kind of secrecy and betrayal doesn't come out of nowhere. It is born out of years and years of financial miscommunication. We're willing to bet that this guy and his current wife have been arguing about money since the day they got married. They've probably argued about his ex-wife too. Maybe the new wife resents that part of their income has to pay for his alimony. Maybe he's tired of having to make both women happy and paying off his ex seemed like a quick way to cut his losses. Maybe he didn't tell his current wife because he's used to making all the financial decisions and it didn't occur to him to tell her.

The *why* here is their money personalities. It could be that he's a Spender and she's a Security Seeker. That's why they've had a history of financial miscommunication. But miscommunication isn't financial infidelity—lying because you want to avoid communication is. This man had a choice about *what* to do about this payment: tell his wife or hide from his wife. And he chose to hide. That's when the financial infidelity happened, right there, with that decision.

This section is going to take you through a process of looking at your *what* moments. What decisions have you made as a result of the financial conflicts in your relationship? What behaviors have you taken on to avoid future conflicts about money?

These are questions that require tremendous introspection and honesty, but we promise that the hard work that's ahead of you will pay off. Until you acknowledge the way your decisions have impacted your relationship, you simply can't break the cycle of financial infidelity. It will keep happening until either you resign yourself to a relationship devoid of any kind of financial partnership or you are divorced.

Toxic Secrets

We see it all the time. A couple comes in with a huge financial mess. We talk to them about how they got to this place, and they have no answer. But then one of them will say, "The reason we have no retirement is that she spends all of our money." Pretty soon they unravel their history: When they first got married she killed their budget decorating their first house, and he got mad about it. That's why she stopped telling him how much she spent when she went shopping. But he pays the bills and found out anyway and that's why he doesn't trust her. She got her own credit card so she could spend money without having to answer to him. He found out about that, too, and now he *really* doesn't trust her. Little secrets, small deceptions, minor attempts to control each other, and white lies—these are the seemingly benign behaviors that add up over time and turn toxic. When one partner finds out the other one has been lying—and they always find out—the level of trust in that relationship goes down. Even when those lies amount to little more than shaving a few bucks off the true price of a purchase, they can tear into the trust that holds a relationship together.

When one partner exerts too much control over the other partner, she is making it clear that there was never much trust to begin with. She controls the finances because she doesn't believe her partner can manage them. So with every financial decision comes a little blow to the confidence of the person being controlled. Before long, that person has become totally disengaged from the finances and the relationship.

And when a couple fails to talk about money at all, when both partners find themselves deep in debt with no idea how they got there or staring retirement in the face with no plan in place, there is a temptation to start blaming. They will blame each other, blame the in-laws, blame their jobs. They will turn on each other and destroy their relationship because neither of them is willing to accept responsibility for the mess they've made.

The math is simple: differences in money personalities can lead to conflict, and conflict can lead to financial infidelity. When couples don't talk, don't communicate, and don't accept each other or extend grace to each other, that infidelity becomes toxic.

Your Turning Point

The walls that go up in relationships are built one brick at a time—one secret, one lie, one half truth, one effort to control. These bricks build up until a couple is living in two different worlds. And they have no idea how it happened. This chapter is going to take you through a list of questions we call the Financial Relationship Index (FRI). We developed the FRI to help couples assess how tall those walls have become. It is meant to help you find the *what* in your financial infidelity. *What* have you been doing that is contributing to the problems in your financial relationship? You will be asked to name specific behaviors, specific choices you have made that have gotten you where you are right now.

The way we see it, you have three options at this point:

1) Take the FRI, even though it will mean uncovering perhaps years of secrets and betrayal, and get your relationship moving in a better direction.

2) Decide it's not worth it and call the lawyer to end this relationship.

3) Keep doing what you've been doing—lying, hiding, not talking about money—and see where it gets you. If you're anything like the majority of our clients who choose this option, you'll end up divorced—in practice if not on paper.

If you choose option #1, we have to warn you: the next few chapters are going to be brutal.

But if you are ready to keep going, if you're ready to invest in your relationship, then the rest of this book is going to help you do just that. Start by looking each other in the eye right now and saying, "I am willing to do what it takes to make our relationship work." Then take the FRI. Work through the questions and be brutally honest with yourself. You're not going to tell your partner about your answers just yet. All you need to do right now is go through the FRI and have your partner do the same. After you go through the questions, you'll figure out your score. That score will indicate how severe the problems are.

Once you get your score, take some time—a few days, even a week—to digest what you've learned about yourself and your financial relationship. Then move on to the next chapter. That's where we will work through your results on the FRI and start moving you into the process of recovering the trust and honesty that may have been lost, but are the core of effective financial communication.

If there are huge issues here, such as long-term patterns of deception and betrayal, you might need to pick one or two areas you want to focus on first, rather than trying to solve these complex problems in a few weeks. If what you have to discuss with your partner feels like it could cost you your relationship, we suggest you work with a marriage counselor as part of this recovery process.

No matter what the FRI reveals, there is hope for your relationship. We know couples who have worked through these questions and revealed secrets they'd been keeping for decades, couples who, with a lot of work and commitment and grace, have recovered and rebuilt strong, healthy partnerships. If you're ready, you can be one of those couples too.

The Financial Relationship Index

Nearly every couple has some degree of struggle in their financial communication. But few couples have a sense of how serious—or innocuous—those struggles are. We only know our own experiences. So if you and your partner argue less about money than your parents did, you might think you're doing great when in fact you actually argue about money more than you need to. Or you might have friends with a marriage that's falling apart because of financial infidelity and you feel like you're doing pretty well because you only fight about money when the credit card bill comes. Or maybe you feel like all you do is argue about money when really it only happens once in a while.

We worked with an expert in statistical analysis to develop the FRI. It gives you the chance to look at your relationship on its own, without comparing yourselves to anyone else. You're just looking at your behaviors and habits so you can assess the quality of your financial communication.

Here's how it works. Each of you needs to complete the FRI on your own. So get a piece of paper and a pencil and head off by yourself for a bit. Answer the questions as honestly as you can—the more honest you are, the more prepared you will be to deal with the financial issues in your relationship. Remember, you don't have to show your answers to your partner until you're ready, which might be a few weeks or even months from now. The goal is to find out your level of financial infidelity so you have a realistic sense of what the issues are in your relationship and how you'll need to address them.

Take the test, then calculate your score using the key on pages 93–94. Once you have your score, and have shared it with your partner, you are ready to move on to the next chapter to find out what you can do to deal with financial infidelity.

THE FINANCIAL RELATIONSHIP INDEX[1]

1. How often do you and your partner discuss money?
   a. Daily   b. Weekly   c. Monthly   d. Yearly   e. Never

2. How often do you and your partner fight about money?
   a. Daily   b. Weekly   c. Monthly   d. Yearly   e. Never

3. How often do you purchase items in secret?
   a. Daily   b. Weekly   c. Monthly   d. Yearly   e. Never

4. How often do you lie to your partner about what an item did or will cost?
   a. Daily   b. Weekly   c. Monthly   d. Yearly   e. Never

5. Do you buy gifts for other people without your partner's knowledge?
   a. No   b. Yes

6. Do you have a secret stash of cash?
   a. Yes   b. No

7. Do you have a credit card that your partner is not aware of?
   a. No   b. Yes

8. How much do you dread talking to your partner about money?
   a. Don't dread   b. Slightly dread   c. Dread

9. Do you look over and pay your bills together?
   a. Yes   b. No

10. Do you or your partner have an allowance?
   a. No   b. Yes

11. Do you as a couple have a joint or separate checking accounts?
   a. Joint   b. Separate

12. How stressed are you about finances?
   a. Not at all stressed   b. Slightly stressed
   c. Stressed   d. Very stressed

13. Have you ever had counseling—either personally or as a couple—about your finances?
   a. Yes   b. No

14. Would you ever consider ending your relationship due to your finances?
   a. I would never end a relationship over money.
   b. I would slightly consider ending a relationship over money.
   c. I would separate over financial infidelity.
   d. I would permanently separate or divorce over financial infidelity.

15. Did money ever cause problems or disruptions in your parents' relationship when you were growing up?
   a. No   b. Yes

16. How much total credit card debt do you have as a couple (be sure to include any debt you brought with you into the relationship)?
   a. $0—5,000   b. $5,000—10,000
   c. $10,000—20,000   d. $20,000—30,000
   e. $30,000—and above

17. Are you comfortable with the amount of debt you as a couple have?
   a. Very comfortable   b. Somewhat comfortable
   c. Not comfortable   d. Very uncomfortable

18. Do you and your partner agree on a budget?
   a. Yes   b. No

19. Do you and your partner have a plan for your retirement?
   a. No   b. Yes

Now go to pages 93–94 to calculate your score.

Financial Relationship Index Answer Key

Question 1
If you answered a, give yourself +0
If you answered b, give yourself +1
c. +1
d. +2
e. +3

Question 2
a. +5
b. +4
c. +3
d. +1
e. +0

Question 3
a. +8
b. +6
c. +4
d. +2
e. +0

Question 4
a. +8
b. +6
c. +4
d. +2
e. +0

Question 5
a. +0
b. +4

Question 6
a. +8
b. +0

Question 7
a. +0
b. +5

Question 8
a. +0
b. +2
c. +4

Question 9
a. +0
b. +5

Question 10
a. +0
b. +3

Question 11
a. +0
b. +5

Question 12
a. +0
b. +1
c. +3
d. +5

Question 13
a. +0
b. +4

Question 14
a. +0
b. +4
c. +6
d. +8

Question 15
a. +0
b. +4

Question 16
a. +0
b. +2
c. +4
d. +6
e. +8

Question 17
a. +0
b. +1
c. +3
d. +5

Question 18
a. +0
b. +4

Question 19
a. +4
b. +0

Your Score:

0–25: You have very little financial infidelity in your relationship. And that's fantastic. At the same time, remember that all it takes is one little lie, one little secret, to send your relationship into a spiral of deception. We don't say that to scare you, but to let you know that even if things are going pretty well right now, it's worth incorporating the advice in the coming chapters into your financial communication. Building healthy habits when things are good can go a long way toward preventing them from ever going bad.

25–50: You have developed some faulty communication patterns, some bad habits, and maybe even a few secrets that are keeping you from having honest financial conversations. The good news is that it won't take a ton of effort to get yourselves unstuck and moving into a much stronger financial relationship. The chapters that follow will give you a solid plan for doing just that.

50–75: You are on the road to disaster, but you're not there yet. There's still time to hit the brakes and turn this relationship around. It will take some serious work from both of you. You'll need to start thinking about the reasons you are hiding your spending or setting up secret accounts. And if you want to heal your relationship, you'll need to prepare yourself for the difficult conversations that are about to take place. We will give you the tools in this book, and we believe that if you use them and commit to working through your issues together, you can rebuild your relationship.

75–100: Clearly money is a major issue in your relationship. We'd guess that you either have tremendous conflict over your finances or have stopped talking about them altogether. Even if that's the case, you have done something crucial by reading this far. You have demonstrated hope. And that's huge. We believe every relationship can be saved from financial infidelity— including yours—with time and true commitment.

You might find that the issues you need to work through are just too much for the two of you to manage. If that happens, we urge you to not only use the tools in this book, but to find a marriage counselor, a therapist, a member of the clergy, or another relationship professional who can guide you through the process of rebuilding a relationship that has been badly broken.

Chapter Five

Confronting the Causes of Financial Infidelity

*C*ongratulations on getting to Chapter 5. At this point, you have determined your personal Financial Relationship Index (FRI) score and your partner has done the same. You both know exactly what kind of financial infidelity you've been up to and what you're ready to talk about. But before you do that, we want you to read through this chapter so you are completely prepared to have an honest, productive conversation.

Remember, the FRI is meant to show you the *what* in your financial infidelity. It pinpoints the behaviors that you've been using to avoid having real, honest dialog with your partner. We've found that those behaviors fall into five basic categories of financial infidelity:

- Overspending and debt (FRI questions 16, 17)

- Financial separation (FRI question 11)

- Lack of planning (FRI questions 18, 19)

- Control (FRI questions 8, 9, 10)

- Secrets (FRI questions 3, 4, 5, 6, 7)

You might have scored high in some of these areas and low in others. You might have scored low across the board or maxed out on all five. No matter what your score, you can overcome these issues and forge a new path of healthy financial communication.

> *You need to know that you are absolutely not alone in your struggles.*

As you do, you need to know that you are absolutely not alone in your struggles. We have seen so many couples who think they are at the end of the road only to find that there is still a way out of the mess they've created. As long as you are both committed to working through your issues and making genuine changes in your financial relationship, you can turn the *Titanic* around.

People, Not Processes

Most of the financial advice out there does a great job of laying out plans and processes for getting your budget back on track. But we've found that until a couple deals with the problems in their financial *relationship* and decides to end their bad habits once and for all, those plans are useless. That's why the truly hard work of repairing your budget comes right here, before any charts or calculations, in the conversations you have and the decisions you make to improve your financial communication.

The overspending, the separate accounts, the lack of planning, the controlling, and the hiding are problems that impact your finances, to be sure. But they are also signs that you have a severe deficit of the basic elements of a healthy relationship: forgiveness, grace, trust, and a sense of shared responsibility and purpose. Without those elements in place, even the most perfect budget plan on the bookshelf won't help.

The focus of this chapter, then, is on you and your partner, on the ways financial infidelity has infected your relationship. Your FRI results tell you which of those five areas you need to work on. This chapter is going to tell you how to work on them.

With your personal scores in mind, read through this chapter. Pay attention to the areas where you know you're struggling. When you're done, we're going to send you on a date of sorts where you'll sit down and talk about which of these issues is creating the biggest problems in your relationship. Then it's up to you to determine how much detail you want to go into about each issue.

Here's our advice: If you want to truly get to the bottom of these problems, you'll need to allow yourself to be pretty vulnerable. You'll need to prepare yourself to hear things from your partner that you might not want to hear. And you'll need to offer a level of honesty that could be uncomfortable for you. It won't be easy, but it is the only way to start over and rebuild your financial relationship.

Overspending and Debt

Charlotte came in to see Bethany a few months before she and her boyfriend got married. She had done a great job of saving over the years and had a solid head start on her retirement. She was worried because her fiancé, Taylor, had about $20,000 in credit card debt. Charlotte told Bethany, "He has a problem with spending, but I think it will be OK once we get married."

Of course, it wasn't. Charlotte was a Security Seeker and Taylor was a Spender. Because they didn't have that basic understanding of their different approaches to money, they didn't have any idea of how badly their money personalities could clash. And clash they did. Charlotte assumed that Taylor would follow in her financial foot-steps once they were living together. Taylor just kept doing what he had been doing his whole adult life—spending money—and with Charlotte's income added to his, he had more to spend!

Charlotte and Taylor never talked about their financial partnership. Charlotte never talked to Taylor about his debt, never asked how he'd gotten in so deep. She'd never asked him to work with her to develop a budget that would help them pay off his debt while still maintaining some savings and investments. What she did do was fume in silence as Taylor blew through her savings and ruined their credit rating.

> *Debt is without a doubt the number-one issue for most of the couples we talk to.*

Debt is without a doubt the number-one issue for most of the couples we talk to. Whether they've been married for fifty years or are getting married in fifty days, these couples are stuck in a cycle of spending and debt that they simply can't get out of.

For some, it started before they even met each other. One partner came to the relationship with a few thousand in student loans. The other came with a few thousand in credit card debt. They got together and suddenly they are nearly $10,000 in debt without having spent a dime as a couple.

For others, the rude awakening comes when they want to refinance their house or get a home improvement loan or buy a car and they discover that they have $40,000 in debt. They have no idea how it happened. They didn't go out and buy a boat; they just lived life and racked up some serious debt.

Some money personalities don't worry about debt, but for others, like Security Seeker Charlotte, it creates a kind of instability they find almost intolerable. So they start reacting to the spending, to the debt, by trying to control the person who is spending, or trying to restrict the budget to pay down the debt. If there's no communication about these decisions, each person's money personality kicks into high gear and the clashes become inevitable. And that's when the financial infidelity starts.

Charlotte tried giving Taylor an allowance. Naturally, he resented this. He felt like a child when she suggested he get her approval on any purchase he made. When he showed up at breakfast in a new pair of shoes or came home with a new gadget from the Apple store, he knew Charlotte would give him her scowl of disapproval and he hated it. He already felt like a kept man because Charlotte made more money than he did, but her constant spoken and unspoken reminders that he was irresponsible made the situation worse. He resented the control Charlotte tried to have over him, and he responded by spending more, just to show her he wasn't about to live under her rule.

The more Taylor spent, the more anxious Charlotte became. As she watched all her savings trickle away, she started hiding money in their retirement account, hoping she'd be able to salvage something. When Taylor started tapping into that money, she created a new account without his knowledge. Taylor's spending led to Charlotte's hiding. Instead of making a plan for dealing with their debt together, Charlotte and Taylor let the subsequent financial infidelity ruin their relationship.

Restoration

Ending the financial infidelity that comes around when there is overspending and debt involves some readjusted expectations. If you scored high on questions 16 and 17, overspending and debt are likely an issue for you. Recovering from this infidelity involves a concerted effort to work together to solve the problem. Use these tools:

- **Stop the shame and blame.** What we see in the couples we talk to about debt is a terrible shame game. The debt has them so stressed that the only coping strategy they can think of is to blame each other. Charlotte had her mantra: "We wouldn't be in this mess if you hadn't been so irresponsible," and she used it a *lot*. Taylor's response wasn't any better. He'd say, "You don't know how to have fun. If it were up to you, we'd never do anything or go anywhere." They were extremely ticked off at each other and entrenched in their battle. But when debt is the problem, it really doesn't matter how you got there; assigning blame doesn't make the debt go away. What does make it go away is paying it off. Together. Charlotte and Taylor had to get to the point where they could shut up long enough to decide if they even wanted to move forward. As we talked with them, it was clear they did. And the first step on that journey was to stop blaming.

- **Put an end to control.** As Charlotte discovered, debt doesn't go away when you cut up your partner's credit card. It doesn't go away when you give him an allowance. Those moves only make the tension and financial infidelity in the relationship worse. Getting out of debt requires both partners to commit to a plan of action. If there is resentment and mistrust, it's almost impossible to get that kind of commitment. Charlotte had to show some trust in Taylor. She had to stop treating him like a problem child and start treating him like her partner and husband. She had been using her income as a weapon rather than a resource for them to create a life together, and he felt that every time he spent money. Ironically, that lousy feeling compelled him to spend more as a way of trying to feel more independent.

- **Accept responsibility.** Sure, Taylor bore more responsibility for the debt than Charlotte. So what? When you share your life with someone, you share all of it, the good and the bad. Once they were married, Charlotte and Taylor both contributed to the environment that allowed this debt to grow. Even if Charlotte's part was limited to staying silent when she learned about Taylor's debt, she did play a part. Both of them needed to learn how to communicate, how to recognize their part in the problem, and they needed to be prepared to move on.

- **Cast a vision.** Spenders, the money personality most likely to get stuck in this kind of financial infidelity, tend to be very *now* focused. They don't think much about the future debt their current spending will create. In this case, Taylor had spent money on things that gave him instant gratification—vacations, computers, flat screen TVs, etc. He needed Charlotte's planning skills to help him get a vision for their future. When Charlotte explained that the reason she wanted to save money was so they could travel when they retired and have some fun in those years, Taylor began to see that the future could be just as much fun as the present if he was willing to help make it happen.

- **Make a plan.** Charlotte and Taylor worked with Bethany to develop a debt-reduction plan that allowed them to get rid of the debt over the course of a few years while still leaving room for some discretionary spending. Part of that plan included a tighter budget for Taylor, but because he had some input into how this process was put together, he was willing to curb his spending to solve the problem. If you have more than $5,000 in debt, we suggest you meet with a financial planner to create a plan for reducing your debt. Most people can cut back their own budgets enough to pay off smaller amounts, but few people have the skills or discipline to create a serious pay down on their own. Regardless of how you get your plan together, you need to be prepared to make some changes in how you live, how you spend, and how you communicate to make it work. You will need to commit, not only to paying the debt, but to being honest about your spending, trusting each other to stick with the plan, and communicating about how you're doing each month.

Financial Separation

Want to see a relationship that isn't working? Meet Jerrod and Melissa. Jerrod told us, "I usually pay attention to Melissa's account and transfer money accordingly. If I forget, I tell her not to spend money for a day or two. It's nothing more than a casual conversation. She worries that she doesn't help financially, but she's got the kids and that's the most important thing right now."

In some ways, that sounds like a great arrangement. For Jerrod. But what about for Melissa? He transfers money to her account when he decides she needs it? Seriously? And if he forgets, she can't spend any money? Really? And then comes the real kicker—she's got the kids. He doesn't mean in the divorced-parent-custodial sense. He means that's what she does, not what he does.

> *From the finances to the parenting, this relationship is divided right down the center.*

Jerrod and Melissa are living completely separate lives. From the finances to the parenting, this relationship is divided right down the center. He has his world, she has hers, and never the twain shall meet.

Melissa used to feel OK about this arrangement. She liked having Jerrod take care of the finances. She'd never been very good with money and was content to let him make decisions about how they spent his income. But as the children got older and Melissa had a bit more time to herself, she started to feel hemmed in by her allowance. Jerrod had determined how much she should have in her account based on her life as the at-home mother of two small children. But with both of her kids in school during the day, she wanted to explore some of her own interests, maybe take an art class or volunteer for a local charity. The problem was, she had to ask Jerrod for the money to pay the tuition for the class. She had to ask for the money to buy a few professional outfits for charity events. And she felt ridiculous having to explain why these things were important to her. And when Jerrod suggested that she find other, less expensive hobbies, she felt more than ridiculous, she felt angry.

Money personalities play a huge part in this brand of financial infidelity. That's certainly the case for Jerrod and Melissa. He's a Saver; she's a Flyer. He likes to keep a careful watch on his money, and she doesn't really care all that much. So for most of their life together, Melissa has been perfectly happy to let Jerrod have control of the finances. But now, in typical Flyer fashion, she's finding that her lack of access to money is getting in the way of her dreams. And that's a problem for Melissa. She feels like she has to ask for Jerrod's permission and approval before she can explore her passions or interests. And the lack of financial communication between these two is driving them apart.

Restoration

Financial decisions dictate all kinds of other decisions, so when finances are separated, those parts of life that finances impact—which are just about everything—become separate too. And that's not a relationship. Here's how to rebuild a financial relationship in the wake of the financial infidelity that comes with separate finances:

- **Reevaluate your reasons.** We're all for each partner having a sense of individuality. We're all for healthy differentiation between two people. But when it comes to money, separation is nearly always an excuse for a lack of trust. If you and your partner have been maintaining separate checking accounts, separate credit cards, or separate investments, it's time for a serious talk about why you are keeping some or all of your finances apart. You need to talk about why you made this decision. Then you need to figure out if that reason still exists. Jerrod and Melissa had made their decision even before they got married. Melissa had run into a few minor financial scrapes while she was in college. So when they got married they agreed that Melissa would close down her personal checking account and Jerrod would set up an account in her name at his bank. But marriage and motherhood brought out a more responsible, organized side of Melissa. She was not the young woman who didn't understand money stuff. She was an adult who could—and should—participate in the family finances. Once Jerrod and Melissa talked about the ways they had changed, they both knew it was time to rethink their financial arrangement.

- **Account for your accounts.** It could be that you and your partner keep two checking accounts or two credit cards—one for household expenses, one for work expenses—

because it makes it easier to do your taxes. Or you have two incomes and it's more efficient for you to keep track of your personal cash flow when you have your own account. We know couples who have separate accounts for just these reasons. But every month, these couples sit down with all of their bills and all of their bank statements and all of their paystubs and they look at all of it together. That's partnership—no secrets, no hiding. The separation exists in name only. Jerrod and Melissa might still decide that it's best for Jerrod to handle the bulk of their finances, especially since Melissa is a Flyer and not all that interested in being the bookkeeper. But they need to set aside time each week to talk about their financial goals and how they can work together to make them happen. If Melissa wants to free up money to take a class, Jerrod needs to help her figure out how to make that happen. And instead of Jerrod deciding when Melissa should get her money—and how much she should have—he has to bring Melissa into that decision and find out what fits her needs. That openness, honesty, and collaboration is the only way to keep separate accounts from becoming separate lives.

- **Let go of the past.** We realize that for some couples, the decision to maintain separate finances is based on a specific breach of trust—one partner *did* run the couple into serious debt, or one of them *did* ruin the couple's credit rating by not paying bills on time. And other couples start their relationships with the idea that it's smarter to have your money and my money than it is to have our money. The only way to recover from that struggle, the one that has you keeping your finances separate, is to work toward trust. And that starts with honesty. When you ask yourselves those questions about why you have separate accounts, you have to be honest. Do you trust your partner? Does your partner trust you? If the answer is no, you need to talk about why that trust is missing. Talk about whatever happened in the past that led to this lack of trust. As Jerrod and Melissa talked through their issues, Jerrod started to realize that not trusting Melissa to make good financial decisions was as ridiculous as her not trusting him to make good parenting decisions. Even though he hadn't been a hands-on parent in those early years, he still loved his children and wanted the best for them. Melissa explained that she felt that way about their finances, that just because she hadn't been involved didn't mean she didn't want to work with Jerrod to build a good life for them and their children. They had to let go of the past. If you and your partner have been living separate financial lives because of a lack of trust, it's time to apologize, forgive, and move on. Stop making today's decisions based on yesterday's— or yesteryear's—mistakes and assumptions. Start moving toward partnership.

Lack of Planning

Here is a situation that we ran into during one of our meetings at our practice. Jerry and Linda had been married for about twenty years when they came in to our offices for the first time. They wanted help chipping away at their credit card debt. So we asked them the first thing we always ask: "What kind of debt have you got?" The answer? $60,000. We asked them how they had gotten into such deep debt and they literally had no idea.

Jerry was a classic Flyer. He was an artist who worked for himself, who had put on his best flip-flops for our meeting. Linda was a classic Spender. She had a corporate job and made quite a bit of money. And she loved to spend that money. She was an elegant woman who dressed beautifully and knew how

We asked them how they had gotten into such deep debt and they literally had no idea.

to present a highly professional image. But they were in a terrible financial state.

The good news was that Jerry and Linda weren't even aware of the financial infidelity in their relationship and therefore weren't mad at each other. They hadn't really clashed about their money issues because Jerry didn't really care and Linda didn't really mind. Because they were mutually clueless, they were mutually unfazed. But the debt was starting to affect their lives and their relationship.

They were getting close to retirement and realized they not only didn't have any money set aside, they owed what money they did have to the credit card companies. They had gotten into the habit of pushing this problem on each other. Jerry thought Linda should handle it since she had a better head for numbers. Linda thought Jerry should figure it out since he had a more flexible schedule and could put more time into it. These assumptions had started to lead to little hints of resentment. Linda became increasingly nervous about Jerry's lack of steady income. She had, for the first time in their life together, started to nag him about his lax schedule and lifestyle. Jerry, who had always thought of money as Linda's thing, started questioning her financial priorities. Did she really need another Armani suit? If she was so worried about the future, shouldn't she be the one to cut back and simplify?

Jerry and Linda weren't on the brink of divorce, but they were on the brink of financial infidelity. The tension was slowly rising. A lack of financial planning brings fear, shame, and blame into a relationship. And the partnership suffers.

Restoration

Since the lack of planning is really about inaction, rather than intentional action, it doesn't take much effort to disrupt this kind of financial infidelity and replace it with healthy financial communication.

- **Look ahead.** Couples who fail to plan have usually failed to dream. So get back to dreaming. Sit down with your partner and reenvision your life together. Talk about new dreams, set new goals, imagine new possibilities. Then create a plan for turning those dreams into reality. Set up a vacation fund or start saving for the pop-up camper you've been talking about. Give yourselves a reason to plan and those plans will be easy to make. Jerry and Linda had settled into a life that felt good to both of them. That contentment was wonderful, but it kept them from making plans and thinking about what life could be like down the road. When they finally started talking about the future, they quickly agreed that their top priority was to travel. Linda's job had kept her from having the kind of long, lazy vacations she longed for. That desire to have the money and time for travel was a huge motivation for Linda and Jerry to make a plan for funding their retirement.

- **Name the tension.** Couples who fail to plan often find themselves dealing with an underlying tension in their financial relationship, a tension they can't quite name.

They don't feel a sense of urgency—there's no crisis as far as they can tell—but something's not right. They feel like they are working hard but have nothing to show for it. They feel like the future is looming and they have no control over what's coming next. They have a lingering sense of fear that they are one financial misstep away from disaster. All this tension and fear can infest a relationship, killing off healthy communication, damaging trust, and creating permanent rifts of resentment. Jerry and Linda came to us as soon as they felt the tension reaching a boiling point. The increased conflict in their relationship was a signal that something was wrong. They needed our help to name it, but they took that crucial first step by recognizing that their arguments seemed to center on money.

- **Deal with debt.** Not every couple that deals with this brand of financial infidelity has the crippling impact of debt added to it, but many do. If you've got debt on your hands, one of the first financial plans you need to make is figuring out how to reduce it so you have the resources to plan for the future. Jerry and Linda had a lot of debt, but they also had the determination to get rid of it. We helped them work up a plan for paying down their debt primarily by reducing their spending. Linda, in particular, had to commit to changing her spending habits. But having their retirement goals in mind gave her plenty of motivation to cut back.

- **Start paying attention.** We know that for people dealing with this kind of financial infidelity, the lack of interest in or commitment to finances is the reason they are in this situation to begin with. But getting your financial relationship back on track doesn't mean you need to become an accountant. It just takes a few simple shifts in behavior to get a handle on your money. The first is to track your income. Linda and Jerry didn't know exactly how much they made every year. Jerry's income fluctuated, and Linda usually had various bonuses that changed her income from year to year. They couldn't create any kind of budget until they knew what they had to work with.

> *It just takes a few simple shifts in behavior to get a handle on your money.*

Then, track your spending. If you're anything like Jerry and Linda, you might have never had an actual budget. You've just spent what you had and figured it would all work out. Well, it hasn't. Instead of winging it, figure out what you actually spend. For the next month, write down every cent—cash, checks, and credit cards—that leaves your pocket. You have to know where your money is going before you can work out ways to save any of it. Once you do, you can figure out where to cut back so you can pay down your debt or start a retirement fund. The bottom line is that solving this problem means taking ownership over your finances. Once Jerry and Linda decided to step up and take control of their financial future, it didn't take a whole lot of effort to get rid of the financial infidelity that had crept into their relationship.

Control

A few years ago we met with Jackie and Jerome. Jerome had been a developer for twenty-five years and had built half of the town they lived in. Jackie had worked a part-time job as a guidance counselor. It didn't bring in a lot of money, but she had loved working with students. And she loved that her schedule allowed her to spend time raising her own children. Because Jerome was the big moneymaker in the family, he felt like he should be in charge of their finances. Jackie didn't mind at first, but it didn't take long for her to feel like Jerome made most of the financial decisions without her. When they wanted to buy a house, Jerome vetoed Jackie's top choice for one he thought would be a better investment. When they planned family vacations, Jerome usually picked a place that coincided with his work-related travel rather than someplace the family actually wanted to go. Jackie tried to tell herself she was lucky to go on vacation and buy a house in the first place, but Jerome's total control over their financial decisions just didn't sit well with her.

Jackie wanted to be more involved in their finances, so she suggested they work with a financial planner—that would be us—to make some decisions about their future. Jerome agreed to come in, but he didn't see any point in talking to us. It was a waste of everyone's time. No matter what suggestions we had, Jerome shot them down. Every question we raised—even the truly innocuous ones about how much they made—got his defenses up. Before long, Jerome walked out of the meeting, leaving Jackie feeling defeated and embarrassed.

The last straw came when Jackie started working full time. Two months after she made the change, Jackie tried to use her credit card, only to find it declined. She wrote a check for her daughter's band camp and the check bounced. Jerome had driven his company—and his family—into terrible debt. He had used the family income to pay off creditors from work. He had hoped that he could replenish the money with a quick real-estate deal, but that fell through and he had nothing. Jackie had no idea what he'd been doing. She was financially devastated. But when Jerome suddenly asked for a divorce and left her and the kids, you know how she responded? She said, "Thank God my husband left. I am finally free!"

You know something has gone horribly wrong in a relationship when divorce feels like a gift from God.

We know far too many couples like this, couples where one partner wants to have total control over the finances. And whether that person decimates the funds like Jerome or runs the family business with an iron hand, having one partner in control creates the kind of relational imbalance that makes financial infidelity so dangerous.

If you're the person in your relationship who feels controlled, then you know this section is for you. But if you're the person doing the controlling, you might not realize—or want to acknowledge—that something needs to change. So here's how you know if you are taking too much control over your finances: if you worked through the FRI and ended up believing that the financial communication issues in your relationship are your partner's fault, then you are probably being controlling.

This kind of financial relationship damages both partners. It is paralyzing for the person being controlled. She loses huge chunks of confidence, of identity. We know a couple where the wife is the controlling partner. No matter what her husband says or does, she poo-poos it. For every idea, every opinion he has, she has some comeback. We've watched him slowly shut down over the years. He doesn't even bother to express himself anymore because he's learned that what he says doesn't matter. He has checked out of the partnership because he can see that she doesn't have room for him. He has no purpose. That's a feeling that sucks the life right out of you.

One woman told us about her daughter and son-in-law. She said, "My daughter's husband controls all of their finances. He gives my daughter an allowance every month. He thinks he's being responsible. She thinks it's demeaning and controlling. She opened her own credit card so she could pay for household expenses without having to go through her husband. Well, he found out about it and was furious. Now he says he doesn't trust her, and she certainly doesn't trust him. They are constantly screaming at each other over money, and they have even become violent. They are now separated and talking divorce."

But control hurts the person doing the controlling as well. The more control she tries to exert, the less control she really has. When the person being controlled shuts down, he stops listening; he stops caring what the controlling partner has to say. The communication stops, the sex stops, the conversations about the kids stop, everything stops. And the controlling partner is left completely alone— maybe not in a physical sense, but in a relational sense.

> *This form of financial infidelity does more than destroy the emotional connection in the relationship.*

This form of financial infidelity does more than destroy the emotional connection in the relationship. It opens the door for all kinds of other acts of financial infidelity. The person in control might be tempted—like Jerome—to do what he wants with the money, knowing his partner will likely never find out. The person being controlled might start hiding money and setting up secret accounts so she can leave. And when she leaves, the only person who couldn't see it coming is the one who has been trying to control everything.

Restoration

Believe it or not, reading this book together is a huge first step toward regaining the balance in your financial relationship. If your partner is the one in control and has agreed to read this book with you, if he or she has taken the FRI and is now committed to talking through its ramifications, then that person deserves your praise right now. Really. Right now. Even though you might not see any change for a while, the fact that the person in control is willing to try means you are already building a stronger, healthier partnership.

It's a huge step, but it can't be the only step. Both of you will need to make some serious changes in your behavior if you want to work through the control issues. Start with these steps:

- **Drop the illusion.** Control is never really control. It's possible to dictate the behavior of another person, but only for so long. Eventually, the person being controlled will push back, even if it's through secret spending and hidden accounts. If you are doing the controlling, you need to know this: You are losing this battle. Your efforts to control your partner are only leading to resentment and secrecy. You have to let your partner into this financial relationship or you will end up with no relationship at all. Ask his opinion, listen to his ideas, treat your partner like you would treat a trusted friend. If Jerome had respected Jackie enough to give her a little input in their financial decisions, he would have found that she had good ideas. And if he had been willing to admit his first bad business decision to her instead of covering it up with worse decisions, they could have worked together to find a solution. Instead, he thought he had to maintain control. And look where it got him.

- **Drop the resentment.** The person who feels controlled needs to know this: You have to choose to let go of the resentment that has built up in you. You have to decide that you are willing to let go of the past and trust your partner. And you have to show your partner that you can be trusted with financial decisions. You need to step up and be a true partner. Jackie didn't ask to be controlled, but she didn't stand up to Jerome's control either. Instead of letting some of his bigger decisions—like the house and the vacations—slide, she could have spoken up, insisted they find a compromise, encouraged him to work with her instead of going solo. But she didn't. That's not to say she deserved Jerome's treatment. But perhaps if she had insisted on being a full partner from the beginning of their relationship, their story might have had a happier ending. The point here is that the partner who is being controlled needs to accept responsibility for abdicating control.

- **Take baby steps toward involvement.** We were doing a radio show a few years ago when a woman called in and said, "My husband won't tell me anything about the budget." We asked her how long she'd been married. She said, "Thirty-five years." We asked her how many times she'd inquired about the budget. She said, "I just did it last week for the first time." If a guy's been doing something for thirty-five years and all of a sudden his wife starts butting in, his first response is probably not going to be one of excitement and joy. No, he's going to tell her to butt out. The partner who has been controlled does need to step up to the plate here, but slowly. It's too late for Jackie and Jerome, but if you are in a controlling relationship, start reconnecting by asking your partner about one piece of the budget at a time. You could ask, "Can you show me what kind of retirement savings we have?" As your communication improves, you can ask about other investments, or ask to help develop the budget item for household or other common expenses.

- **Open the books.** Control leads to secrets, so get rid of the secrets with weekly updates on your financial picture. Even if one person is the family accountant, both partners need to know what's going on with the money (we'll talk you through these weekly meetings in a few chapters). The only way to restore the trust that's missing from this relationship is to start acting like people who trust each other—and like people who can be trusted.

Secrets

This, dear friends, is the magnetic north of financial infidelity; each of the other four areas of conflict we've discussed in this chapter eventually lead here. Excessive debt might be the result of one partner's secretive spending. Financial separation practically begs people to spend in secret. A lack of planning often leads to one partner overspending, which leads to debt, which leads to secret spending. And control? Well, if one person insists on handling all the finances, sooner or later either that person will be hiding something or his partner will. If you had a very high score on the FRI, chances are you are living with a host of financial secrets.

Bethany and I had a couple come in to talk to us before they got married. The guy had never told his fiancée that he had $32,000 in credit card debt. They had been engaged for nearly a year. I sat there as the guy looked at his fiancée and explained that he'd never told her about his debt because he was afraid he'd lose her. And guess what? He did. She felt completely betrayed.

He was a good guy. He didn't mean to hurt the woman he loved. But by keeping this secret from her, he'd shown her that he didn't trust her. He didn't believe she could be his partner and help him figure out a way to deal with that debt. And that led him to deceive her and ruin their relationship.

There are plenty of stories we could tell about the blatant secrets and financial infidelity we see every day. There are stories of women who have set up financial plans for themselves that their husbands know nothing about. There are stories of men who have secret credit cards they use to fund affairs and addictions their wives know nothing about. Those are the obvious stories. And if you're involved in that level of deceit, then this section is about you. But we also meet people who don't think of what they're doing as financial infidelity. They don't think of it as deception. Hannah and Josh had been together for eight years when Hannah came into our office. Hannah was at the end of her rope with Josh's

> *But we also meet people who don't think of what they're doing as financial infidelity.*

lies. She said, "Bethany, I don't know what to do anymore. Josh is spending us into bankruptcy. One of the ways he loves to spend money is to buy things for our son. Every time they go to Target or the mall or anywhere else, Joseph comes home with some little toy Josh has bought for him. Josh and I decided that we needed to put an end to Joseph's expectation that he always gets a toy when we're shopping. We agreed not to buy him anything unless it was his birthday or Christmas. It wasn't even a week before Josh and Joseph came home after running some errands. Joseph came in the door and ran straight to his room. I knew instantly that Josh had bought him a toy and told him not to let me know."

Hannah was stunned that Josh would not only go against their agreement, but would get their child involved in his deception as well. She tried to tell Josh how angry she was, but he blew her off and told her she was making too big a deal out of it.

We find that couples who keep financial secrets from each other, who routinely tell little lies about money, think it's perfectly normal to be less than honest with their partner. It's the everybody's-doing-it mentality. So let us be very clear. It's not normal. It's a violation of the trust your partner puts in you. It doesn't matter if that ignoring comes in the form of spending more than you agreed to spend or using a secret credit card to run up debt on porn sites. Financial deception is financial infidelity at its most insidious.

Restoration

This form of financial infidelity involves layers of conflict. There are issues of control, issues of overspending, issues of poor planning, so putting an end to financial secrets takes a multilayered attack. Here's a start to addressing those layers:

- **Choose your relationship.** To heal the wounds caused by financial secrets, the partner who has been keeping those secrets will need to accept responsibility for his actions and rebuild trust through real change. The partner who has been lied to will need to offer true forgiveness, be willing to accept responsibility for her part in the conflict, and be willing to trust her partner again. None of this will be easy. That's why the first question we ask couples who are living in a sticky web of secrets and lies is this: do you want to solve the problem, or is this relationship over? So we're asking you that same question. Is your relationship worth saving? Are you truly willing to change your habits? If you can't figure out why you should save your relationship, then thanks for reading and we wish you all the best. But if you chose to make it work, then you have made the biggest step toward healing you can make.

• **Don't go it alone.** The deception and loss of trust that come with money secrets can damage a relationship so severely that even your very best efforts won't always be enough to help you truly move forward. So even if you are ready to give up on your relationship, we want you to consider seeing a marriage counselor before you see a lawyer. We've provided some resources in the back of the book to help you find one.

• **Clear the air.** It's essential to make a fresh start with just three words: "I'm sorry for . . ." When one person offers a sincere apology for the ways he has hurt the other, it's like a pinprick in the deep stores of anger, resentment, and disdain. They don't disappear, but they begin to trickle away. That word *for* is an essential part of a true apology. When someone says, "I'm sorry *if* you felt offended," or, "I'm sorry *that* you got angry with me," those aren't apologies. Josh had to look Hannah in the eyes and say, "I'm sorry *for* lying to you about my spending." Hannah had to look Josh in the eyes and say, "I'm sorry *for* getting so angry when you were honest about your spending. I know that made it harder for you to tell me the truth." That's how you apologize. You take responsibility for your actions. That kind of apology opens the door to honest conversation.

- **Get to the root.** Financial secrets don't just happen. They are a response to something—a lack of trust in the other person, fear, a need for more control or more freedom. That doesn't mean the secret-keeper can blame the other person. It means there is tension in the relationship that needs to be talked about. We had Josh and Hannah ask themselves a few questions: Why is there financial infidelity in our relationship? Why did one of us feel the need to keep secrets from the other? What will it take to rebuild the trust in our relationship? Their answers actually surprised them both. Josh felt Hannah had a stronger relationship with their son than he did. Because he is a Spender, Josh expressed his love for Joseph with little gifts and toys. When Hannah tried to put a stop to it, Josh was afraid he'd lose his connection with Joseph. Listening to Josh, Hannah realized that Josh was trying to protect his relationship with their son and not just being sneaky. Together, Josh and Hannah talked about her concerns about their spending and came up with all kinds of nonmonetary ways for Josh and Joseph to strengthen their relationship. That conversation also reminded both of them that they had a great family that they wanted to save. They agreed that they wouldn't let money issues destroy something so precious.

- **Remember your money personalities.** Secrets are often the first lines of defense when two money personalities collide. But one partner's thriftiness or love of spending is not an excuse for the other partner's lies. Instead, use what you know about money personalities to muster some understanding and compassion for your partner. Hannah knew Josh loved to buy gifts, so she asked him to be in charge of birthday and holiday shopping. They'd agree on a spending limit, and then Josh could spend away! Josh, knowing Hannah was a Saver, recognized that he needed to respect her need to have a secure financial foundation. Instead of hiding or fudging, he had to be honest about his spending so they could work together to adjust their budget when he spent more than they expected. Josh and Hannah learned that you have to be willing to step into your partner's money shoes for a bit if you are going to walk down a new path together.

As you've read about the five main areas of financial infidelity, you might have been thinking, *We're not as bad as that couple. Maybe we don't have a problem.* But here's the thing: those "bad" couples started out like you. They started with a little lie, a little debt, a little control, and those little things snowballed until they became the avalanches you see in their stories. So whether your snowball is just a few flakes or a whole snowman, you need to change what you're doing, find a new way of communicating about money, and reclaim your financial partnership. In the next section of the book, we're going to show you just how to do that.

SOMETHING TO TALK ABOUT

Sit down with your partner and complete these sentences:
I am sorry for . . .
I forgive you for . . .

Starting *Again*

Chapter Six

Eight Simple Rules for Fighting Fair

*Y*ou have come so far and we know that six months from now, a year from now, two years from now, you're going to look back at the time you've spent reading this book and working through the issues in your financial communication as a turning point in your relationship. As difficult as it might be right now, it will be worth the effort. You have looked your problems in the eye and are ready to send them packing. Now we're going to help you take another step, one that will show you how to stop the lies and the secrets and the controlling and the battles so you can keep moving forward.

Our goal all along has been to save your relationship by helping you stop financial infidelity and develop better financial communication. So the final section of the book isn't going to show you how to create a budget. It's not going to give you a list of rules meant to get you out of debt. That's because your financial issues aren't the result of using the wrong kind of budget or trying the wrong

> *Financial issues aren't the result of using the wrong kind of budget.*

debt-reduction plan. They are the result of financial infidelity and failed financial communication.

We've shown you how to put a stop to financial infidelity. So now it's time to move on to restoring and practicing strong financial communication. All you need to kick this relationship reconstruction project into high gear are the right tools. Once you have those tools in hand, you can create a partnership in which you can work together to figure out a budget that works for you, or make a plan for getting out of debt, or do whatever it is you want to do with your finances.

The Process

The tools you'll discover here are part of a process. *Process* is an important word to keep in mind. It tells you that this project will be ongoing. You won't use these tools once and then throw them out. You will use them over and over as you learn to communicate, take responsibility, and rebuild trust. You will need them every time you find yourselves living out old habits instead of practicing new ones. And you will live out those old habits, but they won't have the power to infect your relationship the way they used to.

Building better financial communication doesn't mean you're never going to have financial problems. It doesn't mean you will never argue about money again. It doesn't mean you're going to be out of debt in three months or three years. What it does mean, however, is that when you have financial problems, you will know how to talk about them and deal with them together. When you do argue about money, you will know how to diffuse the conflict and resolve it together. And when your debt deepens, you will know how to face it together.

Bethany and I have spent much of the last year creating a new side business. It has been a huge financial risk for us—one that made even Risk Taker Bethany a little nervous, so you can imagine what it did to me, the Security Seeker. I freaked out at least once a week, usually in the middle of the night.

I would be lying in bed, wide awake, worrying. When I couldn't take it anymore, I'd whisper, "Are you awake?" to see if I got a response. When I was really worked up, I didn't so much whisper as lean over and tap Bethany on the shoulder until she woke up. So Bethany would open her eyes, and I'd tell her that I thought this whole thing was a bad idea, that I was pretty sure we were going to destroy ourselves financially. If Bethany hadn't understood my money personality, if she wasn't committed to being my partner, she would have said, "You're being a paranoid idiot. Chill out and go to sleep."

But she does understand me, and she is committed to our partnership. So she would say, "I know this is hard for you. It's a little scary for me, too, so I can only imagine how it feels for you. What do you think you're really afraid of?" And I would talk about my fear of failure, of how this business was a big dream for me—for us—and I didn't want it to fall apart. Once I'd shared all of that with someone I trust, someone who is listening and not judging, I'd feel 1,000 percent better and fall asleep.

We have learned how to communicate about money, and that has made our marriage better now than it was at the beginning. We understand each other better, we trust each other more, we are better people because we have worked hard at putting our fears and our selfishness aside so we can be true partners in our finances and our lives. We have made plenty of financial mistakes, but we've made them together. And if our latest deal tanks, it won't take our relationship down with it because we have made this decision together.

That's our hope for you too—that this is the beginning of the best stage of your relationship. We've said more than a few times that money touches everything. When financial communication has turned toxic, everything it touches rots and deteriorates. But when your financial communication is strong and healthy, the strength and health spread into other parts of your relationship as well. Then, even when the stress of living hits hard, even when disaster strikes, you can face it because you are standing together in a lasting partnership.

The Tools

The next three chapters are going to cover three essential tools for building better financial communication: Fighting Fair, the Money Dump, and the Money Huddle. Unlike most tools, you won't really use these one at a time. Instead, they work together to create healthy, effective communication. Fighting Fair will be the tool you use when you want to figure out how to talk about a financial issue. The Money Dump will be your tool for deciding which financial issues you want to talk about and when. And the Money Huddle will be the tool for actually talking about those issues and determining how you will deal with them.

We'll start with Fighting Fair because it is the bedrock of this process. Knowing how and when to argue—and how and when to step away from an argument—can mean the difference between a conflict that turns contentious and a conflict that becomes constructive. If you're like, well, everybody, this is a tool you'll use often.

The Money Dump is a way of prioritizing the issues you want to deal with together. We'd guess that you feel a bit overwhelmed right now. After everything you've read about money personality conflicts and the various kinds of financial infidelity that might be part of your relationship, you probably have no idea where to start in dealing with all of it. The Money Dump will help you figure that out.

The final tool is the Money Huddle. Basically, this is a regular meeting time when you and your partner will talk through your financial issues. Knowing there is time set aside to deal with the questions and concerns and decisions that are a normal part of your financial life can take away a whole lot of stress from your relationship. We'll show you how to use this time to create conversations about money that you might actually enjoy.

These three tools don't have to be used in a particular order. They aren't steps or instructions. They are ways to facilitate financial communication. So you might find that your first Money Huddle devolves into a big argument. That's when you think about what it means to fight fair. You might be fighting about which financial problem to tackle first—your debt or your spending. That's when the Money

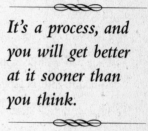

It's a process, and you will get better at it sooner than you think.

Dump comes in handy. So all of these tools get used all of the time. It's a process, and you will get better at it sooner than you think.

Eight Rules for a Fair Fight

It might seem strange for a book about financial communication to include a section on how to fight. Isn't the whole idea to stop fighting? Well, not really. Unless you have some sort of Disney princess relationship going on, you and your partner are going to fight. We do. Our friends do. Every non-cartoon couple does.

The difference between the fights you've been having about your finances and the fights we want you to have about your finances is that these fights won't hurt so much. They won't leave you both feeling bruised and alienated from each other. They won't lead to financial infidelity. Instead, they will actually be part of healthy financial communication. That doesn't mean you should start picking fights. It means that *when* you fight—which we hope will be less often than it has been—you will fight fair.

Rule #1: Commit to Making It Work

Before you read any further, you have to agree to do this. You have to decide you want it to work. Because it won't work if you don't both commit to using these strategies whenever you argue about money. So do that right now. Promise:

- That you will respect each other, no matter how angry you get.

- That you will act like partners in your family business.

- That you will do your best to understand each other and your different perspectives about money.

- That you will show each other grace when you violate these expectations.

  Done? OK.

Rule #2: Start with New Expectations

For you to change the way you fight, you have to change your expectations of each other. The longer a couple is together, the less productive their fights can become. That's because we tend to assume we know what our partners are going to do and say before they do or say it. So we stop listening, we stop responding, we stop trying to understand. Instead, we shut our partners down with words like, "Oh, here we go again!" or, "You always have something to say about that, don't you?" If you really want to fight fair, you have to let go of whatever has gone on before and start fresh.

Rule #3: Diffuse the Situation

This might be the single hardest part of learning to fight fair. It takes tremendous self-control to walk away from a fight. When your blood is boiling, when you feel betrayed or violated in some way, the first response is to lash out and spew out everything you're feeling. It's cathartic to do that, but it doesn't do a thing to solve the problem.

Last winter, we made a decision—together—to sign our kids up for skiing lessons. After all, we live in Colorado and knew that the cost of the lessons would pay off in years of family vacations and day trips to the mountains.

But then I came home from work one afternoon and saw a fax for Scott on the desk. It was the bill for the ski lessons. I don't know what I thought these lessons were going to cost, but I didn't expect them to be $450. I felt the blood rush to my face, and I got ready to call Scott at work and let him know I was not happy about this. Yes, we'd made a decision, but I'd made it thinking we were talking about $200 at the most. To see a bill for more than twice that amount? Uh-uh.

I started to call Scott, ready to rip into him. But then I stopped. I knew I needed to calm down a little so I wouldn't say something I'd regret. I can be a little hotheaded sometimes, and I knew that if I talked to Scott right then, it wouldn't go well. Instead, I waited until I had cooled down and talked to Scott when he got home. There was some tension in my voice—I was still irritated—but I was able to step back from my initial outrage and talk to Scott like a human being, not a raging bull.

Diffusion can be as simple as keeping your mouth shut for a little while. But there will also be times when you need to just walk away. If your partner walks in the door with a pile of shopping bags, even though you have decided together that you're going to cut back on your spending, your first reaction might be to go into a tirade about how she broke your agreement and now you can never trust her again. But instead of undoing all the work you've done already, try telling your partner that you're upset by all those packages and that you want to talk about it after you've had a chance to calm down. And it's OK if it takes you a few hours. It's OK if you have to sleep on it. It's OK if you need to go for a walk or hit the gym or just mutter to yourself for a while.

Diffusion not only stops a heated argument in its tracks, but it can also lead to conversations that deepen your relationship. When your partner comes home with all those shopping bags and you take the time to calm down and then talk about the situation, you might find out that she had a reason for spending what she did. Maybe she got a last-minute call that she's got a big job interview in the morning, one that could lead to a huge promotion, and she needed a new power suit to wear.

And if your partner doesn't have a reason, that diffusion time can give her the chance to realize she's made a mistake. While you're off fuming, your partner might think, *Oh, that's right. He gets really anxious when I spend money like this. I should have talked to him about it first.* By the time you get together to talk about the problem, your partner will have already realized her mistake and be ready to work out a solution.

It may take all the strength you can muster to keep your mouth shut and walk away from a fight. But when you see what a difference it makes in your financial communication, you won't ever want to go back to the impulsive, spiteful habits of the past.

Rule #4: Stay Focused on the Problem at Hand

A fair fight is one that stays on message. When Scott came home on the afternoon of the fax incident, I stayed as calm as I could when I said, "This bill came today and it's a lot more than I expected. Can you help me understand why we're spending this much on ski lessons?"

Because I had let myself settle down a little, I also had some time to think about what was really bugging me. The problem wasn't really the money. It was that I thought we'd agreed to a certain amount and

I wondered why Scott had gone against that agreement. And that was what I needed to talk to Scott about.

It turns out Scott had to make some quick decisions about the lessons, that we had to get the boys in fast if we wanted to get them in at all, and that the bill was for both group lessons and private lessons, one of which we could cancel when we'd had a chance to think through it a bit more.

I could have ruined this whole conversation by bringing up all the other times we've had miscommunication about money. I could have used my anger as an excuse to berate Scott for making decisions without me. But fighting fair demands that we stay in the present. It demands that we deal with the situation in front of us and only the situation in front of us. Dredging up the past only keeps you living there.

Rule #5: Think About Your Money Personalities

Before you read this book, you didn't know how your partner thought about money. Now you do. You understand your partner in a way you didn't before, so use that understanding and empathy to solve your financial disagreements.

As you're talking through your situation, consider how your money personalities have contributed to the conflict. Did you forget that your spending stresses out your partner, the Saver? Did you take a risk without talking to your partner?

> *You understand your partner in a way you didn't before.*

ner? Did you react out of your financial fears? Admit the ways you've let your money personalities get in the way of effective financial communication and do your best to rectify that problem. If the Saver has overreacted, talk about how the Saver can express her fears in a more productive way next time. If the Spender has gone against an agreement you made together, figure out why. If you need to go back to Chapter 3 to review the ways you can solve money personality conflicts, do it.

Your money personality isn't an excuse for behaving badly. It's an explanation for why you think the way you do. But it's your responsibility to express those thoughts and expectations in a respectful way. You can be who you are and still be a kind, loving partner.

Rule #6: Search for Solutions

Diffusing the fight takes a ton of the pressure off the situation. But there are still those shopping bags. Whatever the problem is, you still have to deal with it.

When I came home with my boxes and boxes of home theater equipment and told Bethany that I had spent about ten times the amount we'd agreed on, she diffused the situation by walking away from me and telling me we'd need to talk about this in a little while. It was an oh-boy moment. I knew I had blown it. Actually, I knew it when I checked out of the store. But now I was faced with the anger of my partner, and I knew instantly that we had a problem.

By the time Bethany was ready to talk, I'd already thought about a few solutions. But first, she needed a chance to tell me what she was feeling. Her biggest question was: "What were you thinking? We agreed on $500. This is $5,000." I had to admit that I'd gotten caught up in the home theater experience and lost all sense of reason when Tom Cruise buzzed the tower. So we talked about what to do.

I was ready to just return it all and never go back to the store again, but Bethany reminded me that we still wanted a system, just not a top-of-the-line system. And she was right. I could take the $500 subwoofer back and get the $200 version. I didn't need all the hi-def bells and whistles. I just needed a sound system. I went back to the store, did my exchanging, and we ended up with a perfectly fine system. More importantly, we ended up with a perfectly fine relationship. Bethany felt listened to and respected, I had the system I wanted, and now we can watch TV without both of us feeling totally bitter about our sound system—or each other.

We've found that most financial problems can be resolved when a couple works together to come up with a few possible solutions. So when you're stuck in a financial mess, sit down, talk through your feelings about the situation, and then come up with three or four realistic options for dealing with it. Choose one and make it happen. Purchases can be returned; investments can be reworked. There is very little in the financial world that can't be redone in a way that works for both partners.

Rule #7: Expect to Blow It

We certainly don't expect you to fight fair every time you argue—we don't. But when you mess up, apologize, forgive, and move on. You have spent years practicing lousy financial communication. It's going to take time to unlearn that style of communication and replace it with one that works. So be patient with each other, keep trying, and promise to do better the next time. You might only get it right 30 percent of the time. But that's 30 percent more than you were doing

We certainly don't expect you to fight fair every time you argue—we don't.

before. And that's something. Count that a success and move on. If you get stuck in the failures, you'll never improve your financial communication. Focus on your successes.

But you will, of course, fall back into those old habits now and then. When you do, when you blow it and yell at your partner and say things you regret, you can still diffuse the situation. You can apologize for what you've said. You don't have to apologize for being angry or frustrated. But you can apologize for what you did with that anger and frustration. When you show that kind of humility and maturity and love for your partner, even your missteps can help rebuild trust between you. You are showing your commitment to being a changed person. And that commitment will cover a multitude of mistakes.

Rule #8: Extend Grace

Fighting fair comes down to this: letting go of the past and starting over, every day. We know there is pain in your financial relationship, that there have been terrible mistakes made during your life together. But if you want your relationship to work, you have to be willing to stop using the past as a weapon and start being a person of grace.

There will be times when your partner does something that pushes every button you have, and you will be tempted to lash out in those old ways. But where did those reactions get you? Into a relationship tainted by financial infidelity. If you repeat the same old patterns, you're going to end up in the same old place. We think you want more for yourself and your relationship.

Fighting fair is truly an art form. You won't do it perfectly at first—and maybe never. But you can get better at it, conflict by conflict, week by week, month by month. When you start to struggle, review these tools and try again.

1) Commit to making it work.

2) Start with new expectations.

3) Diffuse the situation.

4) Stay focused on the problem at hand.

5) Think about your money personalities.

6) Search for solutions.

7) Expect to blow it.

8) Extend grace.

SOMETHING TO TALK ABOUT

What do you need from your partner when you are arguing? Patience, understanding, no yelling? Tell each other what you need to help resolve your financial conflicts.

Chapter Seven

The Money Dump: Getting It All on the Table

*N*ow that you know how to fight, we're going to give you something to fight about. (We're only partly kidding.) The next tool in your financial communication toolbox is something we call the Money Dump.

When you worked through the FRI, you identified the potential—and probably some actual—areas of financial infidelity in your relationship: overspending and debt, financial separation, lack of planning, control, and secrets. Those are big-picture categories for the kind of

> *Now that you know how to fight, we're going to give you something to fight about.*

behavior that erodes relationships. Now that you're aware of those categories and know which ones are issues in your relationship, it's time to dig into them in a more intentional way. And that's where the Money Dump comes in.

The Money Dump is the process of getting everything off your chest. It's your chance to write out the good, the bad, and the really ugly in your financial relationship. It provides a cathartic release of all the anger and frustration and bitterness that have built up over the years. And once you get all of that out on paper, you can start to focus on the places where you and your partner need to work together to rebuild your financial communication.

The Yellow Pad

People often get totally overwhelmed by financial conversations. Again, it's that tie that money has to every other part of our lives that makes it such a highly charged subject. But it doesn't have to be that way. When you come to a money conversation with a clear sense of what you want to talk about and a real desire to work with your partner to find a solution to your problem, financial communication becomes—dare we say it?—pleasant.

We also find that people think they have to have a good grasp of how finances work before they can have effective financial communication. You may think you need to know all about interest and investments and lending rates. But you don't. There are people like us who can help you with the ins and outs of the financial world. All you need to prevent future financial infidelity and replace it with strong financial communication is the willingness to stay calm, respect for your partner, and a yellow pad of paper.

That's because financial communication really starts with you and your yellow pad of paper. Of all the budget plans and books and seminars out there, none of them are as essential to getting your financial life in order as that yellow pad of paper. It is the foundation of your money conversations, the key to figuring out who you want to be as a couple and how you're going to get there.

You're going to use that yellow pad of paper to write down everything that's working in your financial relationship and everything that isn't. Both you and your partner will do this on your own. Like the

FRI, the Money Dump calls for total honesty, so you can't worry about what your partner is writing or get hung up on what she might think about what you're writing. So take your paper and a pencil and go off by yourself for a while. Then, dump, dump, dump.

We're going to take you through the dumping process and then later we'll show you an example of a couple who used this tool to repair their financial relationship. Writing out your financial frustrations isn't hard—it's just putting thoughts on paper. But it can be helpful to see how another couple used this process to get to a better place.

The Lists

You're going to start by making two lists. The first list will be all the positive parts of your financial relationship. For some couples, this will be a nice long list. For others, it might take some serious effort to come up with something. If the only positive thing you can write down is that you have managed to avoid bankruptcy so far, or that you haven't gotten divorced yet, or that you've made it to Chapter 7 in this book, don't worry. It all counts for something. Start with what you have.

The second list will be easy. This is where you write down every little thing that's been bugging you about your financial relationship. Don't temper or evaluate what you write. You don't need to worry about placing blame or thinking about causes. There are no limitations here—your partner isn't going to see this list. So let it all out.

If you get stuck, try completing a few of these sentences:

- Our financial relationship is broken because of . . .

- We need to fix . . .

- When we talk about money I feel . . .

- I'm sick of the way we . . .

When I was growing up, my family served as a foster family for a few young girls. One of those girls is truly a sister to me today. But there was another one who really got on my nerves. Everything she did drove me nuts. We argued so much that my mom finally got sick of it. So she had each of us go to our rooms and write down everything that bothered us about the other one. I wrote pages and pages of complaints, listing every slight, every mistake, every look and move and word that had rubbed me the wrong way.

And you know what? I can't really remember what happened after that. I don't remember how or if we resolved any of the complaints on my list. I do remember my mom telling me that my foster sister's list was quite a bit shorter than mine, which meant that maybe I needed to give her a break and not get quite so worked up over everything. Mostly I remember how good it felt to write all of those feelings down on paper.

In a strange way, I felt heard. I don't know if my mom even read my list. But by writing it, I felt like my feelings mattered, like someone was listening.

That's what this purging process will do for you. There is something so freeing about writing down the pain and the frustration you've been feeling for all these years, and that freedom is going to make the next step a lot easier.

Seth and Amy

Seth and Amy have been together for eleven years. For the most part, they get along fine. But their finances are a mess. Seth is a Saver, and Amy is a Flyer. Early in their relationship, Amy forgot to pay a couple of credit card bills, which led to a lousy credit rating, which led to a higher interest rate on their mortgage, which led to both of them having to work longer hours at jobs they didn't really like so they could make the payments, which led to two tired, resentful people.

The stress of their relationship had led to all kinds financial infidelity. Amy is still not good at keeping track of bills and payments and checks. Seth handles the bills, but he often finds a few lying in a stack of mail that Amy accidentally left in the back of the car or overdraws their checking account because Amy didn't write down a payment she made on her personal credit card. Seth gets angry about Amy's disorganization; Amy gets annoyed with his anger. So Amy spends money without telling Seth, and Seth lies to Amy about how much money they have to keep her from spending.

But now they are ready to start over. They've worked through the FRI; they've realized they need to stop lying and keeping secrets. They want to try to rebuild their financial life together. So they each got out their yellow pads of paper and started writing. Here's what they came up with:

AMY:

POSITIVES

We have a steady income.
We only argue about money when it's time to pay bills.
We still have our house.
We have some money in a retirement account—I think.
We kind of had fun talking about our money personalities.

NEGATIVES

We argue about money when it's time to pay bills.
I'm not very organized about money stuff.
Seth is too controlling about money.
I hate talking about money, and he wants to talk about it all the time.
We work a lot and don't have much to show for it.

We can't afford for either of us to stay home if we have kids, but we can't afford day care either, so no kids.

Seth doesn't trust me.

I'm sick of having to explain everything I spend. I just want to buy a cup of coffee and not have to have some big long conversation about it.

He really ticked me off when he told me it was my fault we have to keep our lousy jobs.

We can't afford for me to go to grad school so I can have a different job.

We seem so stuck, and I hate that feeling.

Seth treats me like an idiot when we talk about money stuff. I'm not stupid, I'm just not obsessed with it like he is.

SETH:

POSITIVES

We make decent money.

I can make most of the money decisions.

We have a decent house.

We have a retirement account.

NEGATIVES

Amy is useless with money.

Amy doesn't have a clue how much debt we have.

I don't know how to talk to her about money without getting mad at her.

I'm stuck in this job because I can't afford to quit.

I need a new car but can't get one because Amy screwed up our credit rating.

She's so irresponsible!!!!!

I'm tired of having to hunt for bills and double-check our accounts because she does such a bad job of keeping track of stuff.

I don't like hiding money from her, but I don't have a choice.

I'm pretty sure Amy's lying to me about money. She acts like she forgets stuff, but I think she's just hiding the truth.

Now that's some serious dumping. Your lists might be shorter than Seth's and Amy's, or they might be longer. They might be nicer; they might be angrier. There's no wrong way to do this. Just get it out.

Setting Priorities

Once you've written out your lists, take a little break. You are still working on your own at this point, so take a walk, work out, have a snack—just do something that will take you away from your list for thirty to forty minutes. We want you to breathe a little and come back to your Money Dump with a fresh perspective.

Now you're going to use your lists to set some priorities for the next six months. You've just unloaded and that can feel overwhelming, particularly if you have decades of betrayal and broken trust to deal with. There's no way you can tear down that whole mountain, but you can start chipping away at it, a rock at a time.

First, look over your list of positives. No matter how short it is, you have something there. And that's important to remember. That something means there is hope for you and your partner. No matter what you've got on that other list, this one tells you that you have done something right. And that gives you a place to start rebuilding.

Looking at that positive list, ask yourself a couple of questions:

- How did we make that happen?
- What does that success tell me about the potential of our partnership?

Write down some of your thoughts about these positive parts of your financial relationship. You're going to talk about these with your partner when you hold your Money Huddle (we'll tell you more about that in the next chapter).

Seth and Amy

When Amy looked at her positive list, she saw that she and Seth were actually on pretty solid footing. They had jobs; they had a house. They were actually better off financially than some of their friends who were living from paycheck to paycheck. When she asked herself how they made that happen, she realized that it was largely due to Seth's careful planning and close watch over the budget. His Saver money personality had been a real asset to their life together. She also started to see that his attention to saving could help them set some new financial goals that might make their lives a little more of what they wanted. Maybe they could save enough for grad school or kids.

When he thought about his list, Seth noticed that for the most part, they had met the financial goals he'd set for them when they first got together. They had managed to buy a house, even if they were paying a little more each month than he liked. And they did have some money put away for retirement. They had made those things happen by planning and having a solid goal. He knew that if they set some new goals—goals that Amy was interested in too—they might be able to get on track again. He remembered that, since Amy is a Flyer, it would be pretty easy to get her excited about dreaming up some plans for their future.

Now to the negatives. Read through your list. You're going to pick two or three of these issues to focus on for the next six months. So which ones are most important to you? Which ones do you think are at the core of your financial communication problems?

It would be great to think you can deal with all of these issues, but we know so many couples who try to tackle all of their problems at once, only to get frustrated after a few months and give up. So the goal here isn't to get rid of everything that irritates you. Instead, the goal is to bring your irritation level from an eleven on a scale of one to ten down to a five.

This is an ongoing process, not a one-shot deal. You can always come back to some of these other areas later. But if you're like most couples, you'll find that as you work on your top two or three issues, as you rebuild your financial communication, the others start to become less frustrating too.

Once you've picked these two or three priorities, you're going to do some thinking about why they bug you and what you think needs to be done about them. The idea is that you need to go into your Money Huddle, having done a little homework and prepared to move forward. So ask yourself:

- What is my part in this issue?
- What is my partner's part?
- How would I like to see this situation resolved?

As you answer these questions, think about everything you've learned so far. How do your money personalities affect the way you feel about this situation? What part do they play in how you've ended up here? Knowing why something infuriates you or leaves you feeling betrayed will help you unravel that problem in a more productive way.

Think, too, about what you learned with the FRI. What kinds of financial infidelity will you need to deal with as you move forward? What are the behaviors and patterns that you've developed over the years to avoid or manage this conflict in your relationship? Everything you've been reading and learning has been building to this: identifying the real issues that are keeping you from having effective financial communication and working together to resolve those issues that have—or will—become acts of financial infidelity.

Seth and Amy

Determining a short list of priorities took some work for Seth and Amy. They were both deeply entrenched in blaming each other for their problems. When Amy looked at her list of negatives, she noticed that most of them were about the way she felt when she and Seth talked about money. She didn't like feeling controlled. She didn't like feeling as though Seth didn't trust her. She didn't like feeling like her life was not her own, that she had no control over her own future. So she chose:

> *We can't afford for either of us to stay home if we have kids, but we can't afford day care either, so no kids.*
>
> *We seem so stuck, and I hate that feeling.*
>
> *Seth treats me like an idiot when we talk about money stuff. I'm not stupid, I'm just not obsessed with it like he is.*

For Amy, these three represented her biggest source of frustration—that they were spinning their wheels and not able to work together to have the life she wanted. And as much as she wanted to blame Seth for all of that stuck-ness, answering the questions about her part in the problem made it clear that she had contributed to the situation by ignoring their money issues.

Seth looked at his list and could feel his own bitterness on the page. It was clear he was really angry at Amy and blamed her for most of their financial problems. For him, figuring out what to do with that anger and finding a way to get Amy on board with their finances became his top priorities. He circled:

> *I don't know how to talk to her about money without getting mad at her.*

And this cluster of complaints:

> *She's so irresponsible!!!!!*
>
> *I'm tired of having to hunt for bills and double-check our accounts because she does such a bad job of keeping track of stuff.*
>
> *I don't like hiding money from her, but I don't have a choice.*

There was some clear financial infidelity in this relationship, and Seth knew they couldn't ignore that if they wanted to start over and get their lives back. As he answered the questions about how they ended up here, he could see that he had placed a lot of blame on Amy. And he was smart enough to know that this probably hadn't helped matters.

Once you create a set of priorities, think about how you want to communicate those priorities and prepare yourself to really listen to your partner's response. Remind yourself of how to fight fair and commit to having a real, honest, respectful conversation about money for the first time. The priorities you've chosen will become the agenda for your first Money Huddle, so before you have that Money Huddle, take a day or two to let your financial frustration settle a bit. Use that time to think about what you've decided to talk about and start imagining how it's going to feel to work out these problems together. Then follow these steps to make one final list:

1) Write down all the positives from your original list and your answers to the questions about how you accomplished those things and the hope you have for the future.

2) Add your priority list, along with any notes to yourself about how you want to talk about these issues, what you need to say, and ideas for addressing them. If you need to write down the rules for fighting fair, do it.

3) Include notes to yourself that will help you have a civilized conversation with your partner—reminders of why you love her, a little doodle of the house you'd love to start saving for, the word *grace* written all over the margins. It doesn't matter if your list looks like an eighth-grader's Social Studies notebook. What matters is that you are now equipped to head into your Money Huddle and start your relationship all over again.

Seth and Amy

With their notes in hand, Seth and Amy set a date for their first Money Huddle. And despite all the tension between them, they were able to talk—for the first time in years—about the life they wanted to have. They remembered why they were great together, remembered all that they'd hoped to accomplish together, and how good it felt when they could talk to each other without blame, shame, or secrets. It wasn't easy, and it wasn't short, but it was the best date they'd had in a long, long time.

The process of writing down what's working and what isn't will allow you to get to the heart of the financial infidelity in your relationship. You can repeat the Money Dump whenever you feel the tension boiling up in your financial relationship. Use it to relieve some of that pressure so you can identify the issues you're struggling with and start thinking about ways to work together to deal with them.

SOMETHING TO TALK ABOUT

Finish this sentence:

I am willing to work with my partner because . . .

Chapter Eight

The Key to Restoring Your Financial Relationship

*I*t's the kind of call you always hope to get. About six months ago, I met with a couple, Andy and Naomi, who were in the deep weeds financially. Bethany and I had met with this couple before, so we knew they had been struggling financially for a while. But we didn't know how bad it had gotten until they showed up in my office ready to end the whole shebang.

Naomi's spending was way out of control, and she was quickly driving them into tremendous debt. Andy was doing everything he could to stop the bleed. He had Naomi on an allowance that she completely ignored. He had cut up her credit cards, and she'd just gotten more. There was financial infidelity of every flavor in this relationship. And neither of them was willing to budge.

During our meeting, it was clear we weren't going to get anything close to a solid financial plan in place unless they dealt with some of this financial infidelity. So I walked them through the Money Dump. They both spewed out problem after problem. He's controlling. She's ruining our lives. He doesn't care. She's only thinking about herself. It was a very heated session, and there were a few times when I had to tell one of them to just be quiet and let the other person speak. I asked them how often they argued about money like this. They answered, "Usually once a day."

Clearly there was a long road ahead for these two. I didn't have much hope that they could hack it. They were so angry, and so stuck in their anger, that I wasn't sure they could find the empathy and grace they'd need to move forward.

But we gave it a shot anyway. I asked them point-blank if they wanted to end this relationship or if they wanted it to get better. There was a long silence, and I truly didn't know what they'd say next. But then Naomi looked at Andy and said, "I want this to work." And that was all he needed to hear. "What do we have to do, Scott?"

We spent the next two hours talking about the tools for better financial communication. We talked through what it means to fight fair. We talked about their fears and their money personalities and their assumptions about money. We hashed out a set of financial priorities. We wrote up an agenda for their first Money Huddle and talked about the importance of taking responsibility and offering forgiveness.

We don't believe for a minute that all of your financial communication problems have been solved just by reading the previous chapters. And we know they won't be solved by the time you finish this one. But now is the time to remember that there has been a significant change in your financial relationship. You are no longer two people who can't talk about money. You are no longer two people with secrets and deception and anger. Now, perhaps for the first time in years, you are partners who are committed to healing your relationship and becoming the couple you have always wanted to be.

> *You are no longer two people who can't talk about money.*

Keep that in mind as you get started with the Money Huddle, your third tool for better financial communication. The Money Huddle will soon become your new best friend. But like any friend, it will take some getting used to, particularly for couples who have struggled with communication in general. So be patient, expect some missteps, and don't give up. We can tell you from experience that the Money Huddle goes from painful to purposeful pretty quickly.

Back in Chapter 5, we talked about the five categories of financial infidelity that we see in couples. We explained that the only way to put an end to financial infidelity is to rebuild trust, respect, and the ability to dream together in your relationship. That's what the Money Huddle is designed to do. It is time you set aside to reconnect, to show your partner that you trust her, that you want to keep moving forward together. As you balance your books and pay your bills and talk about your financial goals, you are slowly healing the places of broken trust. You are demonstrating respect. You are remembering what it feels like to dream.

The Money Huddle isn't just about setting up a budget or making sure you pay off your credit card every month. It is about restoring and refining your financial relationship so that you can live as true partners.

Getting Engaged

We've been doing a Money Huddle since our first year of marriage. But it didn't start out as a financial conversation. It started out as a conversation about the difference between fuchsia and lavender.

When Scott and I got engaged, I was in my early thirties. By then, I had seen too many of my friends turn into bridezillas during their engagements. It was like all the love and the joy of the relationship was crushed by their complete and total obsession with creating the perfect wedding. Most of them arrived at their wedding day stressed out and anxious for the whole thing to be over. That's not what I wanted.

I also didn't want Scott to be one of those guys who gets so aced out of the planning that he has no ownership of the wedding. I wanted him to do more than show up and look good. I wanted him to be involved and invested in the process of planning our wedding.

So I devised a plan. I decided I would only talk to Scott about our wedding once a week. We decided that every Friday night, we would go on a date and that was my time to update him on the plans, to show him the flowers I was thinking about, to pick invitations. I could hardly wait for those Friday dates. I'd show up with my big planning notebook, fabric swatches, pictures ripped out of bridal magazines. And Scott would patiently listen as I debated between various shades of pinkish-purple.

Obviously I was much more into the details of the wedding than Scott, but it was important to both of us that our wedding reflected *our* personalities, not just mine. So we had some honest conversations about which pieces of the day were important to him and which ones he was content to leave in my hands. If I asked his opinion on something, he knew I was genuinely interested. And if he didn't care one bit about whatever it was, he let me know.

The result was a wedding that felt like us. We had a blast that day and we believe it was, in part, because the planning process didn't take on a life of its own.

When we started helping couples develop stronger financial communication, we realized that our engagement model might just work for money conversations as well. Wedding details and money management have more in common than you might think. In both cases, there is usually one person who is way more into the conversation than the other. Both can become all-consuming. Both can create a mountain of stress that neither person knows how to deal with. And both can suck the joy right out of a relationship.

So we thought that if setting aside a specific time for wedding talk helped us survive our engagement, maybe setting aside time for money talk could help couples survive their financial differences. And so, the Money Huddle was born. We've found it's the most reliable tool we have for making sure we both stay invested and engaged in our financial communication.

The Money Huddle isn't brain surgery. It's actually a pretty simple concept: get together once a month and talk about your finances. But when you are dealing with a history of financial infidelity, when every conversation about money turns into an argument, or when you just don't talk about money at all, even that simple conversation can feel overwhelming.

So we're going to break this baby down for you. We're going to start by walking you through your very first Money Huddle, the one where you'll use the priority list you developed out of the Money Dump. Then we'll show you how to transition into a more low-key Money Huddle, the kind you will start having on a regular basis.

As you read through these descriptions, there are a few things we want you to keep in mind:

1) One of you is probably going to be a lot more into the Money Huddle than the other. That's totally normal. It took all my self-control and love for Bethany to not want to rupture my own eardrums when she started talking about centerpieces. But after a few weeks of tolerating our wedding talk, I started to kind of like it. I discovered that I had some ideas about how I wanted the day to go, and Bethany was thrilled to hand me the reins on those plans. That's why the Money Dump is so important. It gives each of you a place to start, a point of investment. Each of you has a few priorities, and the Money Huddle is the means by which you will focus on those priorities. Even if your partner isn't as excited about this as you are, if he shows up and participates, you're getting somewhere.

2) Your money personalities will play a huge part in how each of you feels about the Money Huddle and how you decide to use your time. There isn't a Flyer in the world who is going to get excited about spending an hour balancing the checkbook. Security Seekers could have a Money Huddle every morning and another one before bed just to see how the day's interest rates have impacted their retirement accounts. And the Spenders just want to get to the bottom line: what can I spend? So use what you know about each other to set realistic expectations for what you want to accomplish in your Money Huddles.

3) Remember how to fight fair. If your Money Huddle turns into an argument, don't worry. You know what to do now, so step back and diffuse the situation by walking away for a bit. Maybe you'll need to come back to the Money Huddle the next day. That's OK. When you do, talk through the problem calmly and work toward a compromise. Be gracious and respectful and focus on finding solutions, not rehashing problems.

4) Don't give up. Your Money Huddles might be slow and painful for a while. But whether you are working to undo years of lousy financial communication and infidelity or just trying to develop better communication habits, this will take time. So look for the little ways you are improving your financial communication. Maybe you make it one whole week without lying to your partner about how much you spent at Target. Maybe you get rid of one secret credit card. Maybe you call your partner *before* you buy those fabulous shoes. Those baby steps make a difference. They show your commitment to this process—and to each other. This is a process you'll be involved in for the rest of your lives. Stick with it and we promise it will get easier.

The Money Huddle is all about partnership. Sure, one person can take care of the bills. And yeah, it's a lot more efficient to have a family bookkeeper who balances the accounts and keeps an eye on the investments. But that's not much of a partnership. If you want your financial communication to improve, if you want your relationship to improve, you need to move beyond what seems efficient and start thinking about what will strengthen you as a family.

We see it over and over again: Two really are better than one. When one partner is making all the financial decisions, it almost always leads to some kind of financial infidelity. But when a couple works together, when they set goals for their partnership, when they have clear, honest communication, they can accomplish just about anything they set their minds to.

I ran the L.A. Marathon a couple of years ago. And while Bethany was waiting for me at the finish line, I was at mile 24.2 coming to a dead stop. I hit the wall and I was done. Next thing I knew this guy came up and tapped me on the shoulder. "What's up?" he asked. I said, "I can't move." So this guy I'd never met grabbed my arm and said, "Walk with me." So we started walking. He was telling me about himself, how he lived in Mexico and he'd run this marathon before, and pretty soon we were running. And then we were at mile 25. And then he said, "Hey, man, we've got a mile to go. I'm going to finish. See if you can catch me." And I did.

The same thing happens as you work together to improve your relationship. There will be times when one of you is dragging your feet or falling back into old habits. There will be times when the last thing you want to do is sit down and talk through your credit card statement. But that's when your partner pulls you along. That's when you remember that you want something better than what you had before. That's when you get back on your feet and head toward the finish line.

> *Our Money Huddles have become something we both look forward to.*

Our Money Huddles have become something we both look forward to. No, really. And not just because we are money people. We honestly enjoy the process of looking back at the month and seeing what's gone on. We look at where our money went. We look at money that came in. We celebrate our successes. I might bring in ten new clients one month, something I wouldn't necessarily tell Bethany about in our day-to-day conversation. But when those clients show up as added income to our company? That's worth talking about! Our Money Huddle is our time to talk about how we're doing as a family, what we want the next month, the next year, the next ten years to look like. We wouldn't have those conversations if I were sitting in front of the computer balancing the checkbook by myself.

Your First Money Huddle

The Money Huddle is more than a conversation. Think of it as a combination of a date, a business dinner, and a brainstorming session. You need the time and freedom from distractions that make a date worthwhile, the agenda and focus of a good business meeting, and the willingness to dream that makes brainstorming so much fun.

Here's how your first Money Huddle will go:

1) **Set a date.** We want you to make this first Money Huddle happen within the next week, so if that means you have to skip *American Idol* to fit it in, then do it. This is your relationship we're working on here. It's worth one night without Simon. Set aside a couple of hours—yes, that's a long time to talk about money, but you've got a lot to cover and you don't want to feel rushed—when you can be together without any interruptions.

2) **Get rid of the distractions.** If you have kids, hold your Money Huddle after they go to sleep or before they wake up. We know some couples who get a sitter or set up play dates for the kids on a Saturday afternoon so they can have the house to themselves. Turn off your phones, resist checking e-mail, leave the TV off. This is a time to focus.

3) **Get comfortable.** Find a place to sit where you can look at each other and be comfortable. If snacks will make this a more pleasant experience, have snacks. If a bottle of wine adds some appeal, have wine. If you want soft music in the background, go for it.

4) **Set the tone.** This is the date part. Look each other in the eye, hold hands if you want to, and remind yourselves of why you're doing this. You can say something like, "I love you. We are in this together," or, "I'm so glad we're starting over. I know we can do this." If things have been really bumpy for you, do the best you can, even if it's just, "I've unpacked my suitcase, and I am willing to try this."

5) **Talk through your successes.** This is where your Money Dump list comes in. Tell each other about the financial high points you listed and your thoughts on how you made them happen. The idea is to start the Money Huddle on a positive note. You have reason to be optimistic about your future, and we want you to remind yourselves that there are good things in your relationship you can build on.

6) **Talk about your priorities.** OK, this is where things will get meaty. Do your best to stay calm, to avoid casting blame on your partner, and to be honest about the ways you have contributed to the problem you want to deal with. If you can only get through one priority the first time around, that's OK. You will do this again, and it will get easier. Tell your partner what you discovered as you looked over your Money Dump lists. Talk about why you chose this issue as one you want to work on over the next year. When your partner does the same, try to really listen with the ears and heart of someone who wants to understand this person you love. Since you have both come to the Money Huddle with two or three priorities, talk about how many of them you think you can tackle in the next few months. We suggest focusing on one or two issues at a time so you can see improvement. Take on too much change and you will likely end up frustrated. You might find there is some overlap in your lists—maybe you both want to put an end to the lying or both think it's important to get rid of your separate checking accounts. Work together to figure out what is most important to you as a couple.

7) **Set goals.** Once you've talked about your priorities, do some creative thinking about how you can work on those

issues. Break them down into concrete actions you can talk about at your next Money Huddle. Maybe you agree to go a week without fudging your spending totals. Maybe you promise to go a week without asking about your partner's spending totals. Start with small goals you're pretty sure you can meet. After a few weeks, you will start to notice some changes in your financial communication and your relationship in general.

8) **Schedule the next Money Huddle.** Eventually you will move into having your Money Huddle once a month. But for the next month, we want you to have a Money Huddle once a week. Then, move to a Money Huddle every other week for a few months. When you feel like you have a handle on what you're doing and you feel like you're seeing change in your financial relationship, go ahead and move to the monthly Money Huddle. You can always go back to every other week—or every week—if you feel your progress is stalling out.

9) **Break.** That's it. You did it. You have had a productive, healthy conversation about money. Shake hands, hug, give your partner a big smooch. You have just turned your relationship around.

The Next Money Huddle— And the One After That

Your very first Money Huddle will help you talk about the financial communication priorities you developed out of your Money Dump. Once you've done that, you're ready to get into a regular Money Huddle routine.

You'll find that having a regular Money Huddle takes a lot of the stress out of your financial relationship, even when you're not in the Money Huddle. It's like a big release valve for all the financial tension that can build up and sabotage your partnership. Like our engagement meetings, the Money Huddle gives you a set time to talk about finances so they don't have to be the subject of every conversation during the week. You can save those conversations for the Money Huddle and get back to talking about the kids or how much you like each other or how glad you are that you don't have to talk about money all the time.

Every money personality benefits from the Money Huddle. Security Seekers can relax a bit, knowing they will have the chance to check in on their investments in a week or two. Spenders feel better because they have a better sense of what they can spend each week. Risk Takers can keep their partners involved in their prospects because they are talking on a regular basis. Savers can breathe a little easier because they can see just how much money is coming in and how much is going out and know that their partner can see it too. And Flyers? Well, Flyers benefit from the Money Huddle because it gives them a no-brainer way to be invested in financial communication with their partners. It really is a great tool, if we do say so ourselves.

> *Every money personality benefits from the Money Huddle.*

We're going to lay out the structure we use for our Money Huddle. You can follow it for as long as you need, until you feel like you're ready to branch out a bit. There is no right or wrong way to do this. Well, throwing the checkbook at your partner is wrong. But in terms of the order in which you cover your agenda, it's really your call. Do what works for you. What's important is that you are talking to each other again, you are having conversations about money.

The basic elements of a Money Huddle are:

1) **Tone setting.** Once again, you want to have time when you are free of interruptions. Then, do the look-each-other-in-the-eye thing and tell yourselves you can do this.

2) **Bookkeeping.** We break this up a bit. I organize all the bills while Bethany balances the checkbook. Come up with an arrangement that plays on the strengths of your money personalities. Have the Saver pay the bills while the Flyer looks over the credit card statements to see where you're spending. It used to take us three hours to get through all of this, but now we've got it down to about forty-five minutes. And even though that still sounds like a long time, it's forty-five minutes of sitting next to my wife, working on stuff that's important to our family. Believe it or not, it's kind of nice. The bookkeeping part of your Money Huddle is the time to talk about the money you've spent and the money you've brought in. As you look at the bills, you might notice a charge that you forgot to mention to your partner. Or you might see a payment in the checking account that reminds you that your gym membership is coming up for renewal. The bookkeeping also tells you a lot about how you're doing on the financial priorities you've set. You might see that you aren't saving as much as you'd decided you would. Or you might find that you're able to put more money into your retirement account than you thought.

3) **Successes.** A huge part of the Money Huddle is affirming the progress you're making. Because you are doing this once a week right now, you'll have the chance to talk

about the little changes you see your partner making, and noticing those changes is the best way to make sure they stick. So if your partner has gone a week without lying to you about his spending, tell him how good that feels to you. Ask him how it's felt for him. If you've been trying to hold your tongue about his spending, tell him that you're working on it. Praise each other. Pay attention to each other. Give each other the benefit of the doubt. You are starting fresh here, and nothing helps keep that momentum going like positive feedback.

4) **Goals.** Our favorite piece of the Money Huddle is goal setting. We love having the chance to dream together. So wrap up your Money Huddle by talking about the life you want to be living. Be specific. If you want to take a vacation, talk about it. You are now much more familiar with your finances and can set real goals for making that vacation happen. And have fun with the process. If it's easiest to just make a list of your dreams and stick in on the fridge, great. But you can also get a poster board and put together a collage of images that remind you of your goals, or start a notebook where you write about your dreams as a couple, or get a three-ring binder and collect articles from travel or home improvement magazines that will keep you motivated to stick to your goals. Whatever helps you imagine a better future together, do it. This is also the time to check in on the priorities you set during your first Money Huddle. Talk about how you're progressing. Consider the steps you need to take next and make a plan. Break your goals down into small, achievable chunks. What do you want to have accomplished by your next Money Huddle? What do you

want to accomplish within the next month? Chip away at those goals bit by bit and soon you will be deeply invested in this new way of talking about and thinking about money.

Now obviously you will need to talk about your finances outside of the Money Huddle from time to time. You're not going to wait to tell your partner about your big raise until you get to the Money Huddle—"Hey, honey, guess what happened three weeks ago?"—but you should think of the Money Huddle as the time to go over the details so you don't have to spend time and energy worrying about them the rest of the month.

If you feel like you're getting off track or losing sight of your priorities, or if the Money Huddle just doesn't seem to be going well, start again. Reread the section on money personalities. Do the Money Dump again. Use what you've learned in this book to give it another shot. If you are both committed to making changes in your financial relationship, you can do this.

Andy and Naomi came back to our office two weeks after that make-it-or-break-it meeting and told us that their Money Huddle had been one of the most difficult conversations they'd ever had. And they were so glad they'd had it. They were both still feeling pretty raw, but we could see from the way they talked to each other, the way they sat a little closer to each other, and the ideas they had for moving forward that they had already changed their relationship in astonishing ways.

And that brings me back to the phone call. It came just a few days ago, and it was from Andy. "Scott," he said, "we're doing great. The fighting over money has basically stopped. Naomi is still spending money, but when I think she's spent too much, we can actually talk about it without blowing up. She's even offered to return some stuff after we agree that she overspent. It's pretty incredible."

Andy went on to tell me that he's been doing his part to make their partnership work. He's letting go a little, realizing he doesn't need to control the budget with a clenched fist. He doesn't want Naomi to feel like she's his employee. He wants her to feel like his wife, his partner. He's choosing to trust her, and she's responded to that trust by limiting her spending.

But the part of our conversation that made me really believe these two had started over was when Andy told me, "We were having our Money Huddle on Saturday night, and Naomi said she'd really like to start reducing our debt. She wanted to figure out where we could cut back in our budget to start paying down our credit cards." Naomi, a classic Spender, wanted to reduce her spending and get rid of debt. She wanted to be part of a plan with her partner, a plan she knew was good for their whole family. She was done with financial infidelity and knew her husband was too. They had a brand new financial relationship.

> *She was done with financial infidelity and knew her husband was too.*

When a couple is willing to work together, to bring grace and respect and honesty back into their financial relationship, they can overcome just about anything.

The Rest of Your Lives

You have been on a huge journey over the course of this book. The first step on that journey happened when you opened to page 1 and decided to keep reading. You stayed on the path as you discovered your money personalities and learned to see your partner in a new light. You trudged through the muck of financial infidelity by going through the FRI and figuring out just what had really been happening in your financial relationship. You took the long view of your partnership and saw the importance of rebuilding trust and compassion. And you grabbed onto the tools of fighting fair, getting your financial frustrations out on the table, and working through those frustrations in the safe context of a Money Huddle. You have come a long way. We believe you can keep going down this path of healthy financial communication. And we hope you believe it too.

We have told you some relationship horror stories in this book. But there isn't one of those couples who can't recover if they are willing to commit to real change. Whether you are a new couple who wants to keep financial infidelity from infecting your relationship or a couple who has been together so long that you can't remember a time when financial infidelity *wasn't* part of your lives, the tools in this book will help you get on track and stay on track—for the rest of your lives.

Money is at the root of the vast majority of divorces in this country. When you take away the conflict and the tension that money can bring into a relationship, you have taken a significant step in making sure your relationship doesn't become a statistic.

We want more for you than that. You started your relationship with stars in your eyes and hope in your heart. You *can* get back to that place. If you are willing to put the problems of the past behind you and put your relationship first, you can bring back the dreams you had when you started your life together.

And really, that's what this process is about. It's about bringing you back together so you can live out the dreams you had when you first met. You have what you need to put an end to the financial conflict in your relationship and start rebuilding the life you always wanted.

This book has been a huge step, but it's not the last step. You are well on your way to successful financial communication, but you have to continue doing the work. Keep having your Money Huddle. Keep fighting fair.

And as you do, something surprising is going to happen. Not only will you find yourselves living in a relationship you never thought possible, but you will become an example to everyone who knows you. Your friends will see the change. Your parents will see the change. Your children will definitely see the change. And they will want to know your secret. Go ahead, tell them. Spread the word about financial communication. Be the ones who bring financial infidelity to a halt in the lives of your friends. Help other couples experience the same shift you've been through.

We're proud of you, and we hope you're proud of yourselves. You have accomplished something many couples never even attempt: preventing and even ending financial infidelity. So, well done. Now go ahead, give each other a hug. Hey, go out for dinner, maybe a movie, maybe a weekend away. You've earned it.

Appendices

Money Personalities at a Glance

The Saver
- Gets a rush from saving money
- Is organized
- Doesn't spend impulsively
- Avoids credit card debt
- Is patient about purchases
- Prioritizes spending

The Spender
- Lives in the moment
- Loves to buy for others
- Gets a thrill from the act of purchasing, not the item purchased

The Risk Taker
- Is a conceptual thinker
- Is excited by possibilities
- Loves finding the next adventure
- Listens to her gut
- Is decisive

The Security Seeker
- Is an investigator
- Is trustworthy
- Is willing to sacrifice
- Is prepared for anything

The Flyer
- Is basically content with life
- Is focused on relationships, not tasks
- Is happy to let others handle the finances
- Is not motivated by money

Money Huddle Quick Tips

Once you get into a good routine with your Money Huddle, use these tips for making the money topics a little easier.

- Change the payment schedule on your bills so they are all due at the same time each month. We hold our Money Huddle on the fifteenth of every month, so we changed our payments to be due on the twenty-first of the month. That way we know the companies get their money on time.

- If you have budgeting software you like and use, great. If not, don't buy new budgeting software—yet. It adds a level of potential frustration that you don't need right now. We use those cheap yellow pads of paper and a calculator. Once you've gotten used to keeping track of your budget, you can use software if you like.

- Pay off your highest-interest credit card first. Even if that card has the least amount of debt on it, it's going to cost you the most in the long run. Once you pay it off, consider getting rid of it unless you are confident you can keep paying it off, in full, each month.

- Always shop with limits and lists. Know what you can spend *before* you go shopping, and use your list to stick to that limit. If you're not sure how much to budget for a shopping excursion, do your homework online before you go. Know the prices of what you're buying and plan your spending accordingly.

- If you work, take full advantage of your employer's retirement plan. Many companies have matching contribution programs, so make sure you've signed up for whatever is available. You might save on your taxes too!

- Try to make one extra mortgage payment a year. That extra payment can go entirely to your principal—not your interest—so it might help pay down the mortgage more quickly.

- Negotiate the interest rates on your credit cards, especially those you've had for a few years. Credit card companies are usually willing to come down on their rates for loyal customers.

- Talk about your charitable giving. This is an area where couples often make assumptions about what's important. We find that couples who communicate about their charitable giving usually give more.

- Make sure your family is protected with life insurance. The amount you purchase is up to you, but be sure you have enough to cover the following: your mortgage, any outstanding debts, your children's education, and a year's worth of your combined income.

- If you work, make sure you understand your company's health and insurance benefits. Make an appointment with Human Resources to talk through any questions you have. This stuff can be complicated and confusing, so there's no shame in asking for help.

- Consult your insurance agent or financial planner about your possible need for long-term care benefits. With the increased costs of elder care, you may save a lot of money by getting your policy now.

- Commit to contributing to an education fund for your children. This is not only a good idea for helping them build a better future, but it might hold tax benefits for you as well.

- For more ideas, go to www.themoneycouple.com.

The Money Couple
Answers Your Questions

Q. How do we know if we've got too much debt?

A. The simple answer is that any debt you can't pay off is too much debt. But in reality, most couples will have to take on at least some debt. The problem comes when you get stuck in a pattern of revolving debt where you can pay off one debt only by taking on another. There's no quick fix for revolving debt. The only way to deal with it is to stop spending more than you make. That will take discipline, cooperation, and lots of communication. Get started with these steps:

1) Make a list of all your debt: house, credit cards, car, student loans, etc.

2) Divide the items on your list into two categories: debt we're okay with and debt we're not okay with. Most people are comfortable having a mortgage and a car payment, so those would go in the "okay" category.

3) Review the "okay" category. Are the payment amounts on these debts more than you can manage with your current income? Does paying these debts put you in a tight financial situation? Even if you're comfortable with the idea of having these debts, you need to make sure that the payments you make are appropriate for your budget. If not, you might need to refinance or downsize.

4) Total up your "not okay" category. Then ask yourselves some tough questions: Do we have a realistic picture of our income? Are we trying to live a life that's beyond our means? Which debt can we commit to paying off now?

5) Rework your budget to include a higher payment on the debt you've decided to pay down. If you're not sure how to do this, head to www.themoneycouple.com for a specific analysis of how to reduce your debt and stay within your budget.

Q. I believe you get what you pay for, so I like to buy high-quality products. My husband, however, would rather go the cheap route. How do we find some middle ground?

A. Compromise, compromise, compromise. This is a common problem for Saver/Spender couples, but they aren't the only ones who deal with it. We know plenty of Spender/Spender couples that run into this problem as well. It happens because everyone gives purchases a "perceived value." And we have a perceived value for everything from groceries to cars to houses. You won't have much luck trying to argue someone out of their ideas about perceived value, so instead, work to find some middle ground. Here's how:

1) Agree that a compromise is needed and that both of you will have to be willing to give up your ideal.

2) Consult your budget and talk honestly about what you can afford. Then talk honestly about what you really need. Is this a purchase where quality counts or would a less-expensive version do the trick?

3) Narrow down your options to no more than three choices. Then list the pros and cons of each choice. Include the

emotional and relational pros and cons as well. If a purchase is going to create resentment between you, it's not worth it.

4) Use your list to make your decision. If one of you is still uncomfortable, talk through the process again and make sure you have both been heard—and been listening.

Q. Should we accept financial help from our parents?

A. This is one of the most common questions we get. Couples trying to buy a new home, start a new business, or pay off debt often turn to their families for help. Even when family funds are offered graciously, you need to move forward with caution; family and money can often turn into a real mess. To keep that from happening, follow these caveats:

1) Make sure everyone involved is comfortable with this arrangement. If one of you wants to cut a secret deal with your parents, don't. And if one of your parents wants to cut a secret deal with the two of you—the old "don't tell your mother" arrangement—don't. Remember, secrets always bring trouble.

2) Determine if this is a loan or a gift. If it's a loan, lay out a specific plan for paying it off—payment amounts, possible interest, etc. And talk about what will happen if you don't pay it off. If it's a gift, confirm that there will be no strings attached. If you can't come to an agreement on the terms, don't accept the money.

3) Write out your agreement, have everyone sign it, and make sure everyone has a copy of the signed agreement.

4) Make sure you hold up your end of the agreement.

Q. Should we give financial help to our adult children?

A. This is the flip side of the previous question. As couples reach retirement, offering financial help to your children or grand-children can be a wonderful legacy and can have all kinds of positive effects on your family. But it's also important that you make sure your gift won't have a negative impact on your own financial situation. If you are thinking of making a small loan—a few thousand dollars or so—follow the steps above and make sure both of you are on the same page. If you are considering a larger gift, a financial planner can help you with the details.

Q. Should we allow our teenage children to have credit cards?

A. We have found that there are two ways young people learn how to use credit. 1) They are taught by their parents in a safe, failure-proof environment or, 2) they get their first credit card at the student union and quickly discover they owe some company a lot of money. Obviously, we recommend option 1. We suggest you help your child get a credit card with a low balance when he or she is in their early teens. Then put some real time and effort into explaining how credit works. Train her how to read her statement, explain that interest will be added on if she doesn't pay her bill in full, point out the penalties and late fees that get tacked on if she doesn't stay on top of her payments. You can find more information on our Web site, www.themoneycouple.com.

Q. I found a great investment for us, but my wife doesn't think it's a good idea to risk our money. I don't want to miss out on this, but I don't want to make this decision without her blessing. What should we do?

A. This is a classic case of a Risk Taker and a Security Seeker hitting a roadblock. In most cases both partners are willing to put their money in long-term investments like retirement or a college fund. It's the risky investments that create problems: speculative stock versus a savings bond, retirement savings versus a land deal. But investments don't have to be an either/or. Make sure you have a diversified portfolio with enough low risk investments to offset any losses that might come from the high-risk ones. When couples know how to listen to each other and recognize the ways they are different, they can move toward a compromise pretty quickly. If you have an appealing investment on the table, listen to your partner's concerns about the risks. Show her that you take those concerns seriously by listening and having real answers based on the research and fact finding you've done. And if one of you feels strongly that an investment is a bad idea, then back off. No deal is worth ruining a marriage.

Q. My partner doesn't want to have anything to do with our finances. I hate handling all of it alone. How can I get him interested?

A. We all have situations in our relationships where getting our partners to engage seems next to impossible. But we all know that nagging and complaining rarely helps. In fact, it usually results in the person becoming even *less* engaged. But that doesn't mean you're stuck. There are some effective ways to get your partner to meet you at least part of the way on this.

- Start by talking about the importance of having shared responsibility for the financial part of your relationship. Be honest about how difficult it can be, but hold on to the hope that you can find a way to make this partnership work.

- Find out why your partner doesn't want to talk about finances. It might be that he doesn't have a head for money and gets easily overwhelmed. It might be that only one parent took care of all the finances when he was growing up and he doesn't have a good model for partnership in this area. Or he just might not be interested.

- Ask for your partner's advice on how to get him more involved. Maybe he wants more freedom to take care of bills on his schedule, not yours. Maybe he hasn't really thought about his financial goals and needs to start there before he can muster up any interest. Come up with some concrete steps to take in the next month to help you work together (hint: plan a Money Huddle).

- Divvy up the duties based on who has the interest and the skills for each job. Decide who—one of you or both of you—will:
    1) Pay bills
    2) Balance the checkbook
    3) Work out the budget
    4) Set financial goals
    5) Handle investment research

Q. What's the first step in planning for retirement?

A. Retirement can be one of the most exciting times of your life. After decades of work you can focus on hobbies, family, and one-on-one time together. But if you haven't made plans, retirement can be incredibly stressful—for you and your children. Whether you're 25 or 65, it's essential for you and your partner to have clear financial communication about your retirement plans.

We recommend having two kinds of conversations about retirement: relational and financial. There's a time for realism in retirement planning, but there's also room for dreaming. Here's how to make those conversations productive:

Relational

- Talk about your dreams for retirement. Where do you want to travel? What do you want to do? Where do you want to live?

- Start a Dream Board. Collect pictures or articles about places and ideas that appeal to you and tack them onto a bulletin board that's set aside for just that purpose. When you find yourselves wanting to tap into your retirement for present-day needs, look at your Dream Board and remind yourselves what you're saving for.

- Revisit these dreams over time. Add and subtract as you hone in on the life you really want to be living in retirement.

- Communicate with your children and other family members. Make sure they know you are making plans and tending to your future.

Financial

- Establish a retirement goal. How much do you need to live on? What additional forms of income will you have when you retire? What other financial needs should you plan for? What will it cost you to make your retirement dreams reality?

- Make sure you both understand your employers' retirement plans if they have them. Companies often offer matching contributions and other benefits with these plans. Take full advantage of what is offered. It's a great way to work toward meeting your retirement goals and save in taxes along the way.

- Use a retirement planning calculator (you can find one at www.themoneycouple.com) to determine what percentage of your income you need to save each month to reach the goals you've set.

Q. I came into our relationship with a lot more money than my partner. She brought a lot of debt. How should we deal with the tension our pasts sometimes create?

A. The key to easing this tension is to keep the lines of communication open and have clear expectations about how you will move forward. The first step is to decide if you are willing to think about your money and her debt as "yours" or "ours." That's a crucial part of dealing with whatever financial issues you will face as a couple. Once you agree to act like partners instead of two individuals, you are ready to make decisions about your money. Talk about how best to invest what you have. Make those decisions together so that your partner knows she is more important to you than your money. Then tackle her debt. Make sure you never hold her debt—or the help you've given in paying it off—over her head. If the issues pop up again, talk about them. The worst thing you can do is bury your feelings. Keep talking, keep working, and keep focusing on the partnership you are creating.

Q. How much information should we give our children about our finances?

A. Modeling good financial communication and management is one of the greatest gifts you can give your children. If they see you working out money problems, making financial plans together, and talking through financial decisions, they will have an excellent set of money communication tools for their future relationships. If your family is struggling financially, it's okay to let your children know that money is tight. If your kids are old enough, enlist their help in reworking the budget and finding ways to live on less. You don't need to give them all the details of your financial situation, but knowing you are working on solutions will help them feel more secure than leaving them to wonder what's going on.

Q. We know we should be saving money, but we have no idea how much to save.

A. We encourage couples to use these percentages as they save money:

- Retirement: 8 percent

- Medical: 4 percent

- Savings/Emergency Account: 5 percent

But we also remind couples that no matter how much they want to save, they can only reach these goals by working together. So if 8 percent seems like too much, or not enough, go ahead and change it. Just be sure to make that decision together.

Q. What kind of life insurance should we have? I think we're paying too much in premiums, but my husband is convinced we
need to pay that much to make sure we're covered. How do
we know what we need?

A. Life insurance can be a very emotional investment. No one
wants to think about leaving his family without the resources to
live safely and happily. But that emotion can often lead people
to either put off making decisions about life insurance or pour
so much money into it that they strain their family budget. So
the key is to find the happy medium. First, consider what your
life insurance will need to cover:

- Mortgage

- Three years of income

- $50,000 per child for college

- Credit card debt

- Debt—including car, etc.

- Estate taxes

Once you know roughly what you need, look at your current
policies. Will it cover all of the necessities? Does your employer
offer some coverage, and can you take that with you if you
leave your job? If you need to adjust your coverage, consider
term insurance, which is often less expensive. You can use our
calculator on www.themoneycouple.com to help confirm the
coverage you need.

Q. How do you communicate about a will or a trust?

A. To be clear, a will is a legal document where the court system determines how to disperse your properties at the time of your death. With a trust, you appoint a trustee and transfer your properties to them while you're still alive. You instruct the trustee how to distribute properties upon your death and the court is not involved.

Before you actually get the trust, be sure to discuss the following:

1) Who will be the person who will be "in charge" of this trust if something should happen to you?

2) Who will care for your children?

3) Who will care for you, and at what level of care, should you become disabled?

4) Organize all of your financial statements from all assets and financial accounts. Keep those in the same location as your trust or will so both partners have the information readily available.

Q. How many credit cards are too many?

A. There is no magic number, but as a rule, it's better to have a few cards than a lot of cards. You can build up healthy credit with just one or two cards, so you don't need to keep adding them to create a better credit history. And obviously, it's a lot easier to manage one or two cards than nine or ten. We typically recommend couples have at least two credit cards—one for family expenses and one for business expenses. This makes it easier to figure out business-related tax deductions. We also suggest choosing cards that offer some financial benefit to you such as airline miles, hotel points, contributions to a college fund, or cash back. If you're going to use them, you might as well make them work for you. And keep in mind that interest rates are negotiable. If you are a customer in good standing, you can usually work out a lower interest rate than the one you had when you signed up.

Q. We're getting married in three months. What kind of safeguards should we put into place now to help us avoid money problems in our marriage?

A. The fact that you're asking this question gives you a head start on many couples. This commitment to clear financial communication will help you step into your life together without the money nightmares and financial infidelity that infect so many marriages right from the start. Here are a few conversation starters to help you talk about the way each of you think and feel about money:

- What are your money personalities? (See chapter 2.) How have you seen these work together or conflict in your relationship? What do they tell you about the potential challenges in your financial communication?

- How did your parents treat money? How did they solve— or avoid—conflicts over money?

- Do you want to be a two-income couple? Will either of you want that to change if you have children? How would you make that transition? How would you feel about the changes in your standard of living that could come with a single income?

- What kind of income goals do you have as a couple?

- Do you want to rent or own a home?

- Do either of you stick to a budget now?

- Do you track your saving and spending?

- What mistakes have you made with money?

- What stresses you out about money?

- What is your approach to charitable giving?

Acknowledgments

So much goes into the writing of a book, and so there are many people to thank. We want to start by thanking our parents for their continued support and encouragement. We also want to thank all of the people who contributed to our research for this book by telling us their stories. Your honesty will make a tremendous difference in the lives of our readers. Special thanks goes to the team who made the dream of this book a reality: Randy Smith, Carla Barnhill, Mickey Maudlin, Larry Yonker, and Devlin Donaldson. Thank you for your guidance and wisdom. We have learned so much from you.

Finally—and most importantly—we want to thank Cole and Cade for the joy and inspiration they give their mom and dad every day. We love you guys!

Notes

Chapter 1

1. Damon Carr, "Until 'Debt' Do Us Part," The Carr Report, *New Pittsburgh Courier, City Edition*, Feb. 23–27, 2005, p. C1.

2. Raina Kelley, "Love by the Numbers: Your New Marriage Is Bliss—Until the Bickering over Finances Begins. How to Keep Money from Wrecking Your Home Life," Expert Advice, *Newsweek*, April 9, 2007, p. 48.

Chapter 2

1. You can find a complete description of each money personality and more tools for understanding how they impact you at www.themoneycouple.com.

Chapter 3

1. We lay out all of the money personality combinations at www.themoneycouple.com.

Chapter 4

1. Financial Relationship Index developed by Dr. Kirk Cameron.